MW00436434

Human Nature &
Jewish Thought

LIBRARY OF JEWISH IDEAS
Cosponsored by the Tikvah Fund

The series presents engaging and authoritative treatments
of core Jewish concepts in a form appealing to general
readers who are curious about Jewish treatments of key
areas of human thought and experience.

Human Nature & Jewish Thought

Judaism's Case for Why Persons Matter

ALAN L. MITTLEMAN

Princeton University Press

Princeton and Oxford

Copyright © 2015 by Princeton University Press
Published by Princeton University Press, 41 William Street,
Princeton, New Jersey 08540
In the United Kingdom: Princeton University Press, 6 Oxford Street,
Woodstock, Oxfordshire OX20 1TW

press.princeton.edu

Jacket art: Adam and Eve, illustration from the Sarajevo Haggadah (vellum),
Spanish School (fourteenth century) / National Museum
of Bosnia and Herzegovina, Sarajevo / Photo © Zev Radovan / Bridgeman
Images

Martin Buber quotation from "Elements of the Interhuman," in *Martin Buber
on Psychology and Psychotherapy*, ed. Judith Buber Agassi (Syracuse University
Press, 1999) used by permission of Syracuse University Press.

Rainer Maria Rilke quotation from the first of the *Duineser Elegien* was
translated by Alan Mittleman.

All Rights Reserved

Library of Congress Cataloging-in-Publication Data

Mittleman, Alan, author.
  Human nature and Jewish thought : Judaism's case for why persons matter /
Alan L. Mittleman.
    pages cm. — (Library of Jewish ideas)
  Includes bibliographical references and index.
    ISBN 978-0-691-14947-9 (hardcover : alk. paper)   1. Respect for persons
(Jewish law)   2. Judaism—Doctrines.   3. Theological anthropology—
Judaism.   4. Philosophical anthropology.   I. Title.
  BJ1286.R47M58 2015
  296.3'2—dc23
                              2014033941

British Library Cataloging-in-Publication Data is available

Publication of this book has been aided by the Tikvah Fund

This book has been composed in Garamond

Printed on acid-free paper. ∞

Printed in the United States of America

1 3 5 7 9 10 8 6 4 2

But a man, although he exists as a living being among living beings, and even as a thing among things, is nevertheless something categorically different from all things and all beings.

　　—*Martin Buber*

The clever beasts have already noticed that we are not entirely at home in the interpreted world.

　　—*Rainer Maria Rilke*

Contents

I recall two books from my teenage years. The first, which I read around the time when I became a bar mitzvah, was a best seller by the British science writer Desmond Morris. It was called *The Naked Ape*. It was my initial exposure to a kind of popular literature that tried to understand human beings entirely in terms of their evolutionary descent from earlier primates. I remember being both stimulated and disturbed by the book. It made a great deal of sense to me to see human beings as naked apes. But I couldn't quite see myself, the whole of who I was, in those terms. And by parity of reasoning, why should I have allowed myself to see others in those terms as well? Of course, I wasn't able at the time to formulate the problem so crisply. Yet it was a problem that stuck with me.

A few years later, I read William Barrett's *Irrational Man*. Like many Americans in the 1960s, this book was my first exposure to existentialism. I met Søren Kierkegaard and Friedrich Nietzsche, Albert Camus and Jean-Paul Sartre for the first time. The book captivated me. Its questions and perspectives seemed so capacious, poignant, and profound. It gave a voice to my teenage angst, although it didn't help my relationship with my parents, or for that matter anyone. If Morris taught me that human beings were fully at home in nature—or at least should be thought of as fully at home within the empirical boundaries of a natural world—Barrett taught me that human beings are fully at home nowhere. Or minimally, if they think they are at home, they are fooling themselves. Alienation and absurdity are the order of the day. It is entirely up to us to make ourselves into the kind of beings we want to become. We are on our own.

Issues of their quality or plausibility aside, I sensed that these two books were polar opposites. How to live with the polarity perplexed me.

Although I had dreamed of becoming a scientist, my clumsiness with algebra and dismal showing in high school chemistry scotched that hope. Barrett won out over Morris, so to speak. My later teenage and then college years were full of art, poetry, literature, and philosophy. In my first year of college, I made a quixotic choice to take a course in the Bible as literature. I hadn't taken Judaism seriously, and certainly not the Bible, since my Hebrew school days years before. But in my young adult encounter with that text, particularly with its first book, a world of arresting ideas opened up to me. None of these were theological. I didn't know the word at the time, but now I would say that they were anthropological, in the sense of philosophical anthropology: disciplined thinking about what it is to be human. Although the Bible comes from a time before distinctions between literature and philosophy took shape, it is full of disciplined thought. I found, as a nineteen-year-old student, power and profundity in the stories of Genesis. Why had I been so dismissive of them previously, thinking that they were somehow childish? That course set me on a long journey into the Hebrew language, Jewish texts, and Jewish practice, and eventually into thinking of myself as a Jewish philosopher.

As I grew into a life of Jewish commitment, I didn't leave behind the kinds of question raised by a Morris or Barrett. By taking Judaism seriously, while taking poetry, literature, and philosophy seriously, I was challenged by their inner affinities. I remember taking a two-semester course in college on Ludwig Wittgenstein and at the same time a class on Moses Maimonides's *Guide of the Perplexed*. I wondered how Wittgenstein's understanding of language related to Maimonides's view that human language categorically fails to refer to God. I took a course on science, society, and ethics, where we studied *Sociobiology*, E. O. Wilson's just-published blockbuster. I was intrigued by how Jewish views of sociality, embedded in the legal texts and aphorisms of the Mishnah and Talmud, related to evolutionary views such as those of Wilson. I couldn't keep these domains hermetically sealed off from one another.

I still can't. Whether a virtue or vice, that proclivity is reflected in this book. When Neal Kozodoy of the Tikvah Fund asked me several years ago whether I would be interested in writing a book on Jewish views of human nature for the Tikvah-sponsored Library of Jewish Ideas series, I immediately thought that the project would be most worthwhile if Jewish perspectives could be related to general ones, especially of the sort promulgated by contemporary neuroscience and evolutionary biology. We are awash in contemporary versions of the naked ape. How should we take whatever truth is in them while holding on to, or perhaps for the first time discovering, the truth of older frameworks for understanding what it is to be the creatures we are? I wanted to write a book that would help thoughtful Jews, Christians, secular folk, and others reflect on the perspectives generated by the sciences and philosophy in light of the teachings of Judaism.

I don't believe that Jewish teachings refute scientific ones, nor do I think that science and secular philosophy do away with ancient religion. I agree rather with Wittgenstein, who wrote in his *Tractatus* (6:52), "We feel that even if all possible scientific questions be answered, the problems of life have still not been touched at all." Judaism, of course, has a lot to say about the problems of life along with the human beings who have such problems. What I try to do in this book is give those Jewish voices a philosophical articulation in the midst of an extended conversation with other philosophical and scientifically informed voices. I don't have a settled or doctrinaire view of how science and religion should get along (or not get along); I'm interested in a lively dialogue between them. I'm less inclined to defend a piece of territory than to explore it. Although I argue in these pages for a conservative point of view on human personhood—that is, a vantage point that conserves or preserves its uniqueness as well as value in the natural world—this book has (I hope) an open-ended, non-dogmatic quality to it. I try to keep the conversation alive.

I do think that Judaism has truth-bearing things to say about being human, and am keen to defend its broad outlook against certain trends in our culture that aim to deride, debunk, and caricature religious thought or commitment. These often go by the name *scientism*, an overconfident, ideological application of scientific thought to the whole of life. There is no unanimity about scientism, no bright line demarcating science from scientism. For some avid secular public intellectuals, there is no such thing; scientism is just an insult coined by their opponents to discredit their views en bloc. I do think, however, that scientism is an apt designation for certain debunking, deflationary notions about the nature and stature of humanity. I leave it to the reader to decide whether I am being fair or engaging in special pleading.

I would like to thank a number of people whose guidance, friendship, support, conversation, and love helped me in the writing of this book. Pride of place goes to my family—Patti, Ari, Joel, and Tara—for the delight and wonder they add to my life. The existentialists were greatly mistaken; we are not alone but instead in it together. Next, I would like to thank Michael Notis for his patience in listening to all of my science questions, Lenn Goodman for his comradeship and advice on this book as well as in the work of advancing Jewish philosophy, David Novak for his inspiring example of joining Torah with *sophia*, Penny Rubinfine for her good counsel, Suparna Damany and Dr. Bob Wilson for their superb care during a mid-sabbatical health crisis, Neal Kozodoy for his gracious assistance in simplifying my prose, and the Tikvah Fund for sponsoring a leave of absence from my teaching duties so that I could complete the manuscript. I gratefully acknowledge my academic home, the Jewish Theological Seminary, for granting me a sabbatical and providing an intellectually stimulating place to work. Johannes Brosseder, Isaac Lifshitz, Hartley

Lachter, and Celia Deanne-Drummond along with my students Yonatan Brafman and Lucas Krief gave me valuable feedback on various parts of the manuscript. The students in my spring 2014 seminar, Human Nature and Jewish Thought, at the Jewish Theological Seminary helped me road test and refine my approach. The criticisms and suggestions of the anonymous readers for Princeton University Press helped bring greater rigor to the argument. I thank Fred Appel, my editor at Princeton University Press, for his guidance and support.

This book is dedicated to my teacher and friend Reverend Dr. William A. Johnson, who taught and inspired me as an undergraduate at Brandeis University, and who teaches and inspires me still.

Human Nature &
Jewish Thought

ॐ Introduction

For the better part of the last century, human nature was widely considered to be a misleading idea. Humans, it was said, do not come into the world equipped with anything more than their biological substratum. Their most interesting qualities—their characteristically *human* qualities—derive instead from culture, from the effects of nurture. There is no such thing as human nature, I heard a distinguished sociologist say recently. People are malleable; culture is the milieu in which they are formed.

There are many reasons why twentieth-century thinkers came to this conclusion. The idea of the human being as a *blank slate*, a term going back to John Locke (1632–1704), appealed to the modern sense of possibility. If no fixed essence governed the course of our lives, then we were free to create ourselves in our own chosen image. If categories like race, sex, and class lacked any deep, abiding significance, then we could make of them whatever we wished. If neither nature, nor God, nor the past bound us to a predestined template, then we could become citizens of the future, captains of our own fate. The more lightly human nature weighed on us, the greater the scope that could be given to imagination and hope.

Moreover, as modern history has vividly shown, attitudes and ideologies that sought to fix human nature entrenched an often-unjust status quo. Supposed natural and innate characteristics of women were used as reasons to keep them in assigned, restrictive social roles, economically and politically marginal vis-à-vis their male peers. Allegedly inferior races—a trope going back to the Greeks—were thought of as made for slavery or colonization; higher races bore a supposed white man's burden. Exclusionary immigration policies prevented Chinese, and then southern and eastern Europeans, from coming to the United States. They were purportedly unfit (by nature and subsequently culture) to become equal citizens in our democracy. One could add indefinitely to the parade of horrible conceptions. Most horrifically, for the Nazis, Jews were not only inferior; they were subhuman, a kind of "life unworthy of life." Their destruction was required to ensure the health of the alleged Aryan race, the supposed acme of human nature.

In the face of such prejudice (to use a seriously inadequate word), one can sympathize with the impulse either to banish talk of human nature altogether or think of it not as something discovered but rather as something wholly constructed by ourselves—and hence susceptible to endless amelioration, emancipation, and transformation. Unlike other animals, humans could remake their world and themselves; they could become as creator gods.

And yet human nature is back. Owing to developments in the biological sciences, evolutionary psychology, linguistics, and cognitive neuroscience, and the impress of these disciplines on intellectuals, philosophers, and popular culture, the subject has returned. A century and a half after the publication of Charles Darwin's *The Origin of Species*, biology has fully returned humanity to nature. Our traits, we are told, have evolved to help our species succeed and reproduce within our natural environment. At least in this respect, we are no different from all other animals. For so-called sociobiologists, humans are city builders for reasons not dissimilar to why bees are hive builders: these adaptations best promote our survival. Just as Sir Isaac Newton eliminated the ancient difference between the heavens and earth, showing that the same forces governed events in both realms, evolution is no respecter of the presumed distinctiveness of the human species. Darwinism, if we take its logic to its fullest, can be a great leveler, a "universal acid" as the philosopher Daniel Dennett calls it, in which the exalted image we have had of ourselves dissolves. (But must it? That is a question we will explore below.)

Evolution is hardly the only leveler. Much of the recent conversation about human nature has been driven by advances in genetics, dramatically symbolized by the mapping of the human genome in 2003. Genetics has shown an overlap of 98 percent of the human genome with that of the chimpanzee, our closest primate relative.[1] Exactly what significance we should find in this fact depends to a large extent on what we take the role of genes to be in shaping evolved human traits. It is not controversial to think that a complex neurobiological system like the eye is constructed from a genetic blueprint. It is contentious, or at least unsettling, to think of our moods, faculties, abilities, and intelligence as having a genetic basis. It is disquieting to think that some persons may be more prone to violence and less capable of controlling themselves than others—and this because of their genes (in concert with their early childhood experiences).[2] Do some criminals have a genetic predisposition to criminality? Many of us are disturbed by what such a view of human nature does to our moral assumptions and legal practices. But unsettling or not, behavioral genetics will continue to push into these areas, giving us grounds to think that much of what we find distinctive about ourselves is written into our alleles, so to speak.

Another source of disquiet comes from neuroscience. The idea of the soul departed from scientific discourse long ago. One sees the shift in Locke. Yet the concept of the mind took its place. The cognitive sciences have little regard for the mind, though, at least insofar as it is supposed to have some status distinct from the body and more precisely the brain. Neuroscience seems to have banged the last nail into the coffin of philosophical dualism: the hoary dichotomy between mind and body. For many neuroscientists and their philosophical allies, all that we can plausibly mean by the term *mind* arises out of the neuronal activity of the brain, which for all its extraordinary complexity is, at bottom, a three-pound bit of physical stuff. The "computational architecture" of the mind relies on the brain's "hardwired" capacities for memory, learning, language acquisition, and decision making. The very phenomenon of consciousness is thought by many neuroscientists to be simply an artifact of the brain's biochemistry. Stomachs digest, and brains think; that's what they are adapted to do. Increasingly, "brain" replaces "myself" or "I" in casual speech. An eminent biologist, when recently asked whether she believes in God, said, "Part of my brain does."[3] Is "self" destined to dissolve into "brain"? Will we be able to sustain our sense of ourselves as unique, irreducible *persons* in the brave new world of neuroscience?

The return of human nature as a credible concept is both promising and troubling. Evolutionary biology, behavioral genetics, and cognitive neuroscience lend support to the thesis of an underlying as well as universal human nature. In the words of the evolutionary psychologist Steven Pinker, the human brain, together with its abilities and the behaviors that flow from them, evinces "an astonishingly detailed set of aptitudes and tastes *that all cultures have in common* ... [a] shared way of thinking, feeling, and living [that] makes us look like a single tribe."[4] It's not just the universal human fear of snakes— a useful trait to have evolved in Africa hundreds of thousands of years ago—but the production of poetry and food taboos, the exchange of goods, mourning the dead, grammar, the division of labor, age grading, families, and the use of tools—all of which are universal too.[5] They stem from a basal human nature that we now see more clearly with scientifically enlightened eyes. This is promising because we are both getting closer to the truth and have firm (or at least scientifically plausible) grounds to sponsor our moral belief in the fundamental equality of human beings.

But it is troubling as well since it is not clear where this line of thinking leads with respect to the unique worth of our species. Some have already begun to speak of "unsanctifying human life."[6] If we ought now to speak of a human nature rooted in a human biology that is simply continuous with the biology of all other living things, what, if anything, is special about us? Is our sense that we are special, that we have *dignity*, simply an artifact of perspective? Is it no more than a species-wide gesture of self-aggrandizement (now fashionably called *speciesism*)? Perhaps it is a luxury that the planet cannot afford? Some have started to talk about our geologic era as the *Anthropocene*, the epoch where human action has begun to change the very ecosystems of the planet in potentially catastrophic ways. To be the most successful species imposes heavy costs. Unlike the onetime rulers of the earth, the dinosaurs, who likely perished in the climate change brought on by volcanic eruptions and asteroid impact, we might have the distinction of wiping out ourselves.

Human Nature and Human Persons

How then will we take our sense that we are both a part of nature and apart from it? How are human nature and nature as such related? How are both related to person, the term that springs readily to mind when we articulate what we think we are? Science, as it develops accounts of human nature, embeds human beings, apparently without remainder, in the natural world. As such, it gives us a new way of being at home in the universe. But that way also makes us unsettled. If we are in the end nothing more than "systems of particles," as philosopher Wilfrid Sellars put it, can we still understand ourselves as persons? (And if not, should we not prefer homelessness to our new, robustly scientific way of being at home?)

In truth, we have been unsettled for a long time; the biblical materials assayed in this book attest to that. We have long suspected that we don't fit in—a sentiment that Rilke ascribes to our animal observers in the epigraph to this book. For earlier ages, humans, animals though they were, stood apart because they were endowed with immortal, substantial souls. Although they differed from one another, the accounts of Plato, Aristotle, Maimonides (d. 1204), Saint Thomas Aquinas, and René Descartes all linked human nature to our having a soul within us. Soul talk made good sense, given the science of the day. Yet it is much harder to see how soul talk can find a place in our science, at least as it is presently constituted.[7] Rather than talk about the soul, we might better capture our sense of distinction from nature by pointing to the gap between a third- and first-person point of view. Science allows us to see ourselves as complex natural, physical objects; it speaks about human beings in the third person, momentarily but systematically suspending our familiar sense of ourselves. We are complex living things in a world of both other living and nonliving things. The emphasis is on things. Our native way of speaking, however, assumes a first-person stance; we take what we feel ourselves to be—subjects, selves, persons—as existential bedrock. We are not things; we are persons. Or more precisely, we are things who are also persons. We are beings for whom the third- *and* first-person frames of reference are ineluctable.

Human nature puts this polarity directly before us. When we speak about our human nature, we frame ourselves within a world of forces, processes, mechanisms, and functions—a world of things and causes. When we speak of personhood, we locate ourselves within a world of purposes, intentions, and norms—a space of reasons. Even in conventional speech, talk of human nature points to an underlying causal dimension, where nature impinges on and at least partially determines us. Reference to human nature typically invokes appeals to constraints or excuses. ("What do you expect? I'm only human"; "I'm a pack rat, extrovert, [fill in the blank] by nature.") By contrast, personhood allows a more expansive, open-ended sense of ourselves. Human nature implies limits; talk of persons implies stature. Both are true to our reality.[8] Unless we are stricken by an attack of philosophical conscience, we probably don't worry too much about the different valences of these terms. But if we do notice their polar tendencies, as the new discourse of human nature leads us to do, how should we integrate them? *To talk about human nature, I want to suggest, is a way of speaking about ourselves that gives emphasis to our shared, biological origins, features, and history.* It is to speak in a way that attends to and credits the underlying biological conditions out of which our conscious sense of self has emerged. In a scientific age, we can do no less. We nevertheless must keep in mind that science is one of *our* ways of speaking. It is refined, abstract, and impersonal, but it is still a human form of speech. (What else could it be?) We want to follow science down to get to the deepest truth about ourselves—but we want to do so *as* selves, *as* persons who have an interest in truth. Thus, our scientific project—in this case, the project of ascertaining the truth about human nature—is launched from the perspective of persons who are able to suspend their first-person, familiar perspective, to aspire to a "view from nowhere," in Thomas Nagel's memorable phrase, only to return to a first-person stance enlightened and enriched.

We need to incorporate what science tells us about the complex creatures we are into our older categories. Some of that, as I have suggested, comes rather easily. To have a human nature is to share patterns, traits, capacities, and abilities with other human beings—those "human universals" that anthropologist Donald Brown has cataloged. It is to appreciate one's uniqueness against an underlying background of broad similarity. The claim that there is a human nature entails that human beings, notwithstanding the particularities of cultures and their differentiation in the course of time, share so much with one another that their differences are translatable. We can understand, perhaps at best imperfectly, what we human beings in all times and places have made of our humanity; nothing human is alien to us, for the same deep structures, processes, and polarities inform us all.

But some of what we discover is harder to incorporate. Neuroscience seems to argue against the persistence and stability of human selfhood; the self is a story that our brains tell, as they try to find patterns among inputs. A belief in our (relative) freedom of choice and action seems undermined by neuroscientific studies of mental causation; action seems to be initiated before the brain becomes conscious of it, making the (illusion of) choice an afterthought. It is not at all clear how these features of human nature can be made compatible with our familiar (and essential) sense of personhood.

Against the background of nature per se, how can human nature and our self-understanding as unique, valuable, conscious, morally agentic persons hold together? In my view, while we should look to science to tell us about the history and development of our species, our emergent biological structures and functions, we nonetheless must believe that science cannot be the whole story. The felt gap between scientific explanations, which speak in the language of the third person, the language of things, and the first-person perspective of lived experience, is not just unfortunate or untidy; *it is deeply significant*. It is a clue to what we really are. We are beings who cannot only see ourselves as objects; we must continue, if we are sane, to see ourselves as subjects unable to be eliminated. Unlike a machine, to use Immanuel Kant's language, which has "motive power," a human being has "formative power."[9] A subject, a person, is a center of creative agency, a source of unique action and value. Hence, talk of human nature rooted in the ground of nature as such will always brush a bit against our grain. There will always be a "yes, but.... " We need to speak this way, but we must speak in more than this way. There is a gap between biology and personhood. Yet there is also dependence. What is it like to be human? It is to stand in the gap between nature and culture, biology and individuality; it is to hold on to both poles simultaneously.

These matters, considered from a Jewish point of view, lie at the heart of this book. My goal is a critical conversation between new insights into human nature and old, millennia-old Jewish teachings about human beings. My aim is emphatically not to argue against science but instead to push back against what I see as its abuse. The principal abuse is the diminution of human dignity, which some believe must follow from the full return of humanity to nature. I want to argue for the exceptionality of the human, for the worth, beyond price, as Kant puts it, of human beings. I will do so by trying to show where contemporary thinkers, who draw the nerve of their assertions from the new sciences of human nature, go wrong.

They go wrong primarily, I believe, in their reduction of human personhood to allegedly more basic realities. But as I have suggested, personhood *is* basic; it can't be explained by anything more primal without missing the target. Personhood *emerged* from a natural, biological substratum, from the elements of our human nature. But once it comes on the cosmic scene, it is ineluctable. Any attempt to analyze personhood presupposes its reality. It is, after all, we who are doing the analyzing. If we grant the emergent reality of personhood, then questions about human nature are ordered to it. There is something peculiar going on when scientistic debunkers try to persuade us, appealing to reasons, that reason giving is just an evolutionary sideshow and that persons don't really matter. Philosophers call this a performative contradiction.

Insofar as both personhood and dignity are fundamental to Jewish understandings of what it is to be human, I see Judaism as a powerful ally in the search for a credible and creditable, ennobling yet self-critical account of who and what we are. I therefore try to bring ancient wisdom to modern questions. Using Jewish sources, especially the Bible, its ancient rabbinic commentaries (the Midrash), and medieval as well as occasionally modern philosophical expressions of Judaism, I evoke a conception of human nature in which we can recognize ourselves as persons. I invite readers—Jews, Christians, secularists, and seekers—to consider what it has to offer.

Jewish Ideas

The Jewish tradition has a great deal to say about human nature, both explicitly and implicitly (in stories, laws, poetry, and prayer). "Well, of course," a critic might rejoin. *Any* religious, literary, legal, moral, or cultural tradition (Judaism combines all of these) will be replete with understandings of human nature. But every one of them, our critic hastens to add, will also reflect a prescientific, folk-psychological point of view. No traditional material, especially material saturated with theistic assumptions, is up to the challenge of honestly engaging with modern Darwinian biology or neuroscience. The best that you, the Jewish thinker, can do is to play a divine-authority trump card—which will automatically disqualify you from participating in the conversation in the first place.

I disagree. But the critic does have a point. There is a gap, a large one, between traditional Jewish accounts of human nature and modern scientific and philosophical ones. Although there are scholarly and popular books that present Jewish teachings on this subject, it is not immediately clear how one can use those teachings in the context of a contemporary science-shaped conversation.[10] What, after all, do they really have to say to a person who takes their cues from contemporary scientific naturalism?

This question is hardly specific to Judaism. C. P. Snow spoke decades ago of the "two cultures" of science and the humanities—a bifurcation that all thoughtful modern Western people live with. Nor is it the primary business either of religious people *or* scientists, even religious ones, to reconcile what Sellars calls the "manifest" and "scientific" images of human beings.[11] It *is* the business of philosophers, however. There are those philosophers who hew closely to science and are willing to lose the first-person point of view as well as those who defend and affirm it (without, it should be noted, jettisoning science). With the latter, a Jewish philosopher can make common cause.

This book, then, is an essay in Jewish philosophy. Its focus is not human nature *in* Jewish thought, which would require only a compilation and discussion of Jewish texts bearing on the theme. Instead, it is a dialogue between contemporary perspectives and traditional Jewish ones. Both sides have something to gain from the dialogue; both have something to lose from shunning it. Judaism risks intellectual irrelevance by failing to engage with the challenges of contemporary thought. Contemporary thought risks attenuating its moral seriousness if it ignores one of the sources of Western civilization. From an internal, Jewish perspective, let me make it clear that I do not think that the credibility or dignity of Judaism rises and falls on its conformity with science, nor do I think that science has a monopoly on epistemic authority.[12] I do think that Judaism has rich insights into human nature and human personhood, and that these insights are well served by articulating them in a nonparochial way. I do not presume that Jewish ideas come with any intrinsic authority. The only authority they have is that of reason; they have the potential to persuade.

The charge that Jewish thought has only a divine-authority trump card to play is false. Philosophical expressions of Judaism find the rationality inherent in the Jewish sources and articulate it so that readers can evaluate it on its own merits. Religion, the late Richard Rorty said, is a "conversation stopper."[13] I don't agree. Much of the cultural production of the human race over thousands of years is informed and motivated by religious belief. Even modern secular works, such as Beethoven's Ninth Symphony or Thomas Mann's *The Magic Mountain*, are full of yearning for transcendence and redemption. Performances in concert halls or visits to museums have ritual dimensions. The presence of God, so to speak, is never far from the art, literature, and music of the millennia. Would Rorty claim that no work nourished by religious symbols, doctrines, experiences, emotions, or values is intelligible to us? That we cannot enter into a meaningful dialogue with texts or artifacts that speak out of a religious culture? Why then, does "God talk" among contemporaries shut down a dialogue? If people talk about their deepest hopes, concerns, and commitments, relating them to the ultimate purposes of their life and using the word God to do so, the proper response is to listen carefully and empathetically, not to stop the conversation.

It is no different with overt religious texts. Debunkers, such as Rorty, Steve Stewart-Williams, Richard Dawkins, or Laurence Krauss, insist on starting from the top down. A top-down reading begins with the problematic status of divine existence: if you can't prove that the God of scripture exists, then any religious statement that seems to presume divine existence is unwarranted or nonsensical. Religion is then written off as fantasy because its highest principle, God, is no more than wishful or magical thinking.

This approach to religious wisdom seems to me precisely backward. As opposed to making sure that all our ontological ducks are in a row before we can trust anything a religion says, we should see how its ideas play out in the context of moral and social life, how they gain their meaning by the roles they play.[14] We should begin bottom up with the experience of personhood, and see how it is expressed by the world of religious—in our case, Jewish—ideas. Philosopher John Cottingham aptly calls this approach "the primacy of praxis."[15]

The procedure that debunkers endorse—start with (the dubiousness of) divine existence and disparage everything putatively based on it—sometimes holds in life, but sometimes fails. If you are leaving the house and don't want to get wet, then you can check to see whether it is raining, and if it is, bring an umbrella. The matter can be settled by observation (though it also helps to have a belief in the efficacy of umbrellas). The evidence that would satisfy you is narrowly construed. Unless you are afflicted by skeptical doubts, you will be content with the ontological claim that it is raining now. A more complex case of the pertinence of observation and evidence is one where if theorizing has led you to believe that a certain particle—say, the Higgs boson—exists because its existence would offer the best explanation for a specific phenomenon, you can design an experiment to ascertain whether, in fact, the particle is detectable. This matter can also be settled by observation.

But now suppose that we are trying to make sense of the moral norms of a democratic society. Would we need to ascertain that rights *actually* exist in the same way that rain or Higgs bosons actually do? If rights do not exist in *that* way, would democratic moral norms suddenly become meaningless? Would talk about them be nonsense? Would we not instead think that the concept of rights, rather than naming some empirical reality on which all else depends, is an idea that plays a role in a complex process of evaluation, explanation, and practice conducted by persons? The existence of a right (or duty, obligation, promise, judgment, good, etc.) is not a stand-alone fact or fiction. It is a term that cannot be isolated from the role it plays in a form of life. What we need to do, if we are to be empathetic conversation partners, is enter into that form of life, be open to its rationality, allow its views and values room to breathe. We need to accord primacy to praxis. The search for understanding, contra religion's current cohort of cultured despisers, is not a blood sport; not everything is a competition among rival frameworks.

The appeal to interpretative charity cuts both ways. Traditional Jews might well be bothered by my stance that Jewish ideas, such as humans being created in the image of God, don't come with precertified authority, stamped with the prestige of divine revelation. They may object that too much ground has been ceded to philosophy or science, and that Judaism only survives if its believers/practitioners are insulated from doubt. The steadfast affirmation of belief in the face of a culturally and intellectually corrupt secular world, not the meeting of it halfway, is what the hour demands. I disagree.[16] As persons, we have no escape from the space of reasons. The view that Jews need to retreat from the "conversation of mankind," as Michael Oakeshott called it, and defend Jewish commitments and beliefs from a fideistic bunker, is also a piece of an argument.[17] It appeals to reasons; it conceals a philosophical stance. It is furthermore a weak stance, based on despair. It assumes that Jewish ideas are supported by nothing more than venerable just so stories, and that if you don't believe those stories, such as the creation narratives of the Bible, there is nothing more to be said; the whole tradition unravels. That view in the end agrees with Rorty: religion is a conversation stopper.

Both New Atheists and traditional theists want certitude. Both think that there is definitive evidence that can be brought to bear in support of their positions. And both are unwilling to live without resolution. But certitude is not our birthright, nor does it come easily or cheaply. The desire for certitude arises from within our experience of perplexity, from within the interplay of light and dark, knowledge and ignorance, that always attends our quest for knowledge. The desire for certitude wants to override that interplay. It signals impatience with the shifting balance between the two; it represents a panic for resolution. We need to get over the panic. We can live, fully and well, with a lack of resolution. It's not as if, lacking a certain, firm grasp on ultimate truths, we're prevented from beginning or going on. We make our way toward whatever certainties are possible for us from the middle, moving outward. The form of life that we lead is already saturated with norms, principles, beliefs, and convictions. We don't need the certitude of an ultimate truth, speaking to us as if from the outside. We criticize and revise our principles and beliefs from within. The statement that, for example, a human being is created in the image of God is not equivalent to "it is raining now." There is no outside truth maker for this claim. The "evidence" bearing on the truth of that statement is of an entirely different order. It is up to us to be guided by such an assertion, to respond to it, to make it true in our practice and orientation toward life. Praxis is primary.

Religious claims do not amount to the dogmatic bugbear of the debunkers. We should have the same openness, curiosity, and interpretive charity toward religious texts that we strive to have toward other texts as well as toward scientific theory. It is in that spirit that this inquiry into human nature and Jewish thought is conducted.

Looking Ahead

Working from the bottom up, this is a book about philosophical anthropology, not theology per se. (Pointedly, the modern Jewish thinker Abraham Joshua Heschel called the Bible a book about human beings, not about God.) The philosophical argument will proceed in two steps. The first step is to uphold the legitimacy of the "manifest image," that first-person point of view in which we recognize ourselves as unique, valuable, self-aware, and (to a significant extent) self-determining moral agents. The second step is to encounter the Jewish materials as a rich portrayal of the manifest image and complex contribution to a first-person point of view. The plausibility of this depiction will rely not on the ultimately theistic convictions of the Jewish religious tradition but rather on their bottom-up resonance in our lives as persons.

Chapter 1 focuses on the reality of persons in a world of things. I begin and end with some relevant views drawn from the Jewish philosophers Buber (1878–1965), Heschel (1907–72), and Joseph B. Soloveitchik (1903–93). Framed by the Jewish concerns, I turn to a philosophical exploration of human personhood. I first consider Sellars's classic essay on the scientific and manifest images of "man-in-the-world." Sellars shows how urgent and difficult it is to sustain a recognizable image of ourselves as persons in the face of scientism. With additional help from Nagel and Kant, I argue that persons cannot be conceptually scanted in a world of things. Notwithstanding the explanatory power of science, there is more to life than explanation. Explanation of what we are needs supplementing by a conception of who we are, how we should live, and why we matter. Those are questions to which Jewish sources can speak.

Chapter 2 develops a Jewish response to those questions. Using the motif of the *image of God* as an organizing principle, we will see how the sources address such issues as mind/body dualism, body and soul, the relation of human nature to animal nature, sexuality, birth and death, vulnerability and dependence, and violence and evil as well as selfhood and the relations among rationality, emotion, desire, and imagination.

Chapter 3 explores a key dimension of the portrayal developed in chapter 2—namely, moral agency. Against the hard determinism of modern scientism, classic Jewish sources affirm in a nuanced way the concept of free will. Since these sources have also sometimes endorsed a "soft-determinist" view (sometimes known as *compatibilism*), there is some common ground to be found on this complicated issue. How can we continue to embrace a belief in free will, with all that such a belief entails, and still give credence to the new sciences of the brain that qualify or even negate free will at the same time? Although ultimately Jewish sources must affirm personhood, agency, and moral responsibility, there is more than one simplistic way to do so.

Chapter 4 moves into the political and economic aspects of human nature. Given scarcity and interdependence, what sense has Judaism made of the material well-being necessary for human flourishing? What are Jewish attitudes toward prosperity, market relations, labor, and leisure? What has Judaism had to say about the political dimensions of human nature? If all humans are made in the image of God, what does that original equality imply for political order, authority, and justice? In what kinds of systems can human beings best flourish?

In the conclusion, I return to the theme of the worth or dignity of human life. What are the implications, in the face of the contemporary challenges of biotechnology and scientistic materialism, of a Jewish understanding of human nature and human dignity for our common human future?

CHAPTER 1
Persons in a World of Things

Martin Buber writes of epochs in which human beings feel themselves to be at home in the world, secure in the knowledge that they belong, that they are, for all their peculiarities, a part of nature. Their being makes sense as it fits into an ordered, intelligible whole. Explaining nature explains them. "Man lives in the world as in a house, as in a home."[1] Aristotle, a philosophical biologist, is the first great theoretician of this view. For Aristotle, "Man is a thing among [the] things of the universe, an objectively comprehensible species beside other species."[2] But there are also ages in which human beings feel out of joint; their being is a conundrum to them. They are estranged from their world, and do not know where they belong or how, if at all, they fit in. "Man lives in the world as if in an open field and at times does not even have four pegs with which to set up a tent," as Buber puts it.[3] Saint Augustine, explorer in his *Confessions* of the inner world, discovers this view. The natural integrity of Aristotle's universe no longer obtains, and "the original contract between the universe and man is dissolved. . . . [M]an finds himself a stranger and solitary in the world." A sense of "security in the universe" has

come to an end, observes Buber; man, "who has become inse-
cure, and homeless, and hence problematic to himself," is
seized by fresh questioning.[4] Such an age—and Buber thinks
ours was one—leads to a deepened self-understanding—indeed, a more authentic way of living in the world. We discover
the internal dimension to ourselves that sets us apart from the
rest. We recognize that we are the addressees of our own insis-
tent question, What are we? Buber believes that the view of
human nature glimpsed in a world thought splintered and dis-
integrated is truer than the reassuring "scientific" view of the
natural whole. He thinks that the personal view, founded on a
sense of apartness from the cosmos, grasps humanity in a more
adequate (but still imperfect) way.

There is an irony here. In the cosmic whole, the person is
lost. In personal solitude, the whole is gained. To see human
beings as remarkable yet continuous with the natural world, as
Aristotle did, is to lose the peculiar reality of their personhood. To see human beings as divided against themselves, as
caught between good and evil, between kingdoms of light and
darkness, earthly and heavenly cities, as Augustine did, is to
secure a view where personhood is primary. The irony is that
the former perspective affirms a whole, but scants the significance of the human part. The latter stance, which begins after
the collapse of the world as a natural, rational cosmos, grasps
the person as a unique being, a whole world in itself. For
Buber, any plausible teaching about human nature has to take
the wholeness of the human, anchored in the personal dimension, into account. Wholeness (*sheleimut*) becomes Buber's

criterion for whether a conceptual depiction of human nature succeeds.[5]

Buber's younger contemporary, Heschel, affirms the same criterion. In discussing the time-honored procedure of understanding a human being as a special, perhaps-highest type of animal, Heschel asks, "In establishing a definition of man, I am defining myself. Its first test must be its acceptability to myself. Do I recognize myself in any of these definitions? Am I ready to identify myself as an animal with a particular adjective?" For Heschel, we can get off to the wrong start in the very phrasing of the question: "We ask: *What is man?* Yet the true question should be: *Who is man?* As a thing man is explicable; as a person he is both a mystery and a surprise. As a thing he is finite; as a person he is inexhaustible." Whenever we begin to speak of human nature, we must not forget to speak as well of human personhood. Heschel is thus concerned to set human nature and human personhood at some distance from one another. "Our question is not only: What is the nature of the human species? But also: What is the situation of the human individual? What is human about a human being? Specifically, our theme is not only: What is a *human being?* But also: What is *being human?*" Heschel, then, contrasts human nature with being human—the latter term highlighting our way of being *as* unique, irreplaceable persons. On his account, we gain our personhood, ultimately, through our relationship with God. "I am commanded, therefore I am."[6] Given such a perspective, it is easy to see why he is somewhat dismissive of a category so anchored in the empirical as human nature. Yet if we are to work bottom up, as I have suggested, we must be a bit critical of Heschel's dismissiveness. Human nature must have its day.

Buber and Heschel are right to point to existential concerns as markers of human personhood. They do not give us as much help as we would like, however, in defending a perspective that preserves an image of ourselves as unique personal wholes rather than an ensemble of impersonal parts. They bypass science instead of encountering it head-on. Nonetheless, their perspectives are valuable and can address contemporary debunkers. Consider, for example, the famous (or infamous) remark of Francis Crick, the codiscoverer of DNA: "You, your joys and sorrows, your memories and ambitions, your sense of identity and free will, are in fact no more than the behavior of a vast assembly of nerve cells and their associated molecules."[7] This is a succinct instance of diminishing the whole through reducing it to those parts thought to be most basic or ultimate. Crick implies that our sense of ourselves as persons is in some deep way illusory; it needs to be explained away. We need to wake up and see ourselves as a biochemical house of cards. Our consciousness (of ourselves, others, and the world) bottoms out at a "shifting assembly of active neurons throughout the forebrain that is stabilized using massive re-entrant feedback connections."[8] We are our brains; we are a vast assembly of neurons or more precisely, we are the molecules associated with and composing them.

What gets the last word, on Crick's view, is the human as a system of contingent, biochemical parts and neuroelectric impulses. Yet the curious thing is that *persons*—reasoning, evaluating, reflective beings—are asked to endorse and accept this view. Persons are both presumed and undermined. We are being invited to abolish ourselves to arrive at an allegedly deeper truth about ourselves. And that deeper truth is asserted with the authority of science. The purported truth is that in the deepest sense, we as persons do not exist. But we are being asked, as persons, to reconceptualize ourselves along molecular lines. This is paradoxical, though. It is persons, using reason, who pursue scientific truth, who see knowledge as a value that ennobles and elevates their lives. In seeking to discover and persuade, Crick (and all of us) offer reasons for our views. We appeal to others as reason-giving, reason-accepting subjects, even when, as in the case of scientism, the goal is to persuade us that we are elaborate, computationally sophisticated objects. There is a gap between the project and its addressees. We are being asked, as persons, to eliminate ourselves. Buber's criterion of wholeness or, in Heschel's version, human self-recognition as a "who" not a "what" is lost.

Persons and Particles: Competing Images of the Human

For his part, Sellars struggled with the question of what reality persons have in a world evidently composed of particles. Physics, he assumed, is the most basic, most explanatory science. At bottom, the entities and forces described by physics exhaust the accounting of what really exists. (There is pathos in Sellars insofar as he has both a conviction of a unified, cosmic whole, à la Aristotle, and human homelessness within such a putative whole.) As noted earlier, Sellars frames this as a clash between the manifest and scientific images of the human. The philosopher's task, as he saw it, is to integrate the two. What credence can we give to our manifest sense of ourselves as persons, given a physical world that seems to allow no place for such peculiar entities?

Early human thought, writes Sellars, conceived of all objects as persons. When wind blew, it was because a personlike force decided to blow, bending the branches of a tree-person in turn. The world was enchanted; personhood was everywhere. Out of this archaic conception there eventually developed a manifest image of man-in-the-world in which the category of person no longer included inanimate objects or natural entities but instead only beings capable of recognizing themselves as deliberating, acting, self-motivating individuals. The place of persons in the world shrank, but persons, in their new restricted domain, remained quite real. We saw ourselves in terms of a manifest image as natural beings, embedded in the same causal order as the rest of nature, yet also as beings who act on their own motives and reasons. In the manifest image, we are self-causing agents. We occupy a space of reasons, which are fundamentally different from causes. We apprehend ourselves as beings who think. The rational connections between concepts, formed in minds, are irreducible to associations of perceptions, images, sensory data, and even states of the brain.[9] Perceptions, sensations, "raw feels," and so on, from the point of view of persons, are sensory events stimulated by the environment. But thoughts are different; their associative logic obeys its own laws. Unlike perception or feeling, thought has intentionality (to use the philosopher's term of art); it is "about" something in a way that perceptions and feelings are not. Thought refers to the world. From the viewpoint of a person, then, the mental world has integrity and cannot simply be reduced to those physical events, like neuronal firings, described by science.

Crucially, the manifest image of man-in-the-world entails a *social* dimension. Persons exist within a public world constituted by those who can share the same intentions, particularly toward matters like rights, duties, and obligations. These, too, from the perspective of persons, cannot be reduced to the states of physical systems. The social dimension has its own reality, its own integrity.

The manifest image is not naive; to the contrary, it forms the framework within which most of Western thought occurred until the scientific revolution. (Buber and Heschel as well as the entirety of the Jewish tradition that preceded them are firmly committed to the integrity of the manifest image.) But that image, according to Sellars, stands in stark contrast to the increasingly dominant scientific image. Although the latter developed within the commonsense view that we had of ourselves—that is, within the framework of the manifest image—it is today a *rival* image. Not only is it a rival image, but in Sellars's words, it "purports to be a complete image," one that in principle holds a monopoly on the ultimate truth of what we are.[10] And what are we really? Sellars's reluctant answer is that persons—the objects of the manifest image— are "appearances," while our ultimate constituents, what we must really be, are "systems of imperceptible particles."[11]

Sellars's response is reluctant because, unlike some enthusiastic others—those neuroscientists, neurophilosophers, and
evolutionary psychologists—who reduce mind to brain and
human uniqueness to animal sameness, he is caught between
loyalty to *both* the materialist grasp of reality in terms of systems of particles and the world of experience populated by
persons. Unlike today's scientistic debunkers, he does not
want to dismiss the latter as *mere* appearance, but neither can
he endorse the bedrock status of personhood. The result is the
return of a kind of dualism—a two-tiered view. Science describes and explains. All the sciences that bear on the human,
from biophysics to neuroscience, can in principle describe and
explain the human. But to grasp the human fully is not wholly
a matter of description and explanation. There is something
that must be experienced from within. (Sellars thus reenacts
Buber's drama of Aristotle versus Augustine.)

Sellars looked for something that the impersonal language
of science could not quite capture, and that was the experience of being a moral agent. For him, the irreducibility of the
personal is the irreducibility of the "ought" to the "is."[12] Persons are moral beings. They exist within the framework of
groups, communities, of which they consider themselves
members. Communities exist because their members share
common evaluative and moral intentions. Persons in communities think intentionally about moral actions; to be a person
is to think about rights and duties. Hence, for Sellars, "to
think thoughts of this kind is not to *classify* or *explain*, but to
rehearse an intention . . . . Thus, the conceptual framework of
persons is not something that needs to be *reconciled with* the

scientific image, but rather something to be *joined* to it."[13]
That we see ourselves as moral beings who judge, value, decide, and act exempts us, for Sellars, from a world where causal
explanations, the world of physics, can settle everything. We
live in a world where *reasons* matter; the rest of the world is a
world of *causes*.

The Persistence of Persons

The manifest image sees the category of person as its real, irreducible subject. A feature of this image is that it resists the
objectification of persons into things. The rest of the world, as
if viewed from nowhere, (mostly) opens itself up to scientific
description. Persons are different. We can be described and on
many levels explained, from the molecular to the psychological, at least in principle. But that is not enough. For we are
subjects of our own experience, intention, thought, and judgment, not just objects. We experience what it is to be ourselves
in a unique way. Furthermore, we assert our *value* as persons
in our intercourse with one another as well as in our regard for
ourselves. We resist consistently seeing or evaluating ourselves
as things. We recoil in consternation and disgust when others
view or treat us as things.

Nagel captures how the subject, personhood, cannot be
eliminated with the idea that *thought* as such is irreducible. If
thought were to be explained as a kind of neuronal activity,
such an explanation, illuminating as it would be if it could be
carried through, would nonetheless fall short. If it tried to reduce and locate our personhood at the level of fundamental

physics, it would pretend to locate our being *outside* thought. But as thinking beings, Nagel argues, we cannot get outside thought.[14] The very scientific explanations that purport to tell us what thought, rationality, or consciousness are at the level of systems of particles, what their evolutionary history and purpose are, and so forth, present themselves to us *as* thoughts, which need to be judged, believed, or disbelieved, as do all other thoughts. Try as we might, we cannot occupy a standpoint from which we can regard all our thoughts as psychological manifestations, neuronal electrochemical reactions, adaptive responses selected for by evolution, bourgeois false consciousness, or what have you. The very ability to identify or criticize some of our thinking from one of those perspectives assumes the objective character of some other domain of thought—the domain from which such alleged judgments are made. *We cannot think ourselves to a place beyond thought.* Thought is basic. Persons, in their typical, mature lives, are thinking beings. Personhood, in this respect, is a persistent feature of the world as we know it.

The other half of the equation of personhood, our status as moral beings, as agents who can and must decide and act, is also fundamental and not able to be eliminated. Nagel writes:

> The only response possible to the charge that a morality of individual rights is nothing but a load of bourgeois ideology, or an instrument of male domination, or that the requirement to love your neighbor is really an expression of fear, hatred, and resentment of your neighbor is to consider again, in light of these suggestions,

whether the reasons for respecting individual rights or caring about others can be sustained, or whether they disguise something that is not a reason at all. And this is a new moral question. One cannot just *exit* from the domain of moral reflection: It is simply there.[15]

We are not, as Kant said, volunteers to morality.[16] We can't decide to take it or leave it. It is the medium in which our personhood is exemplified. We cannot escape it, unless we can figure out a way of coherently annihilating our personhood. A debunking argument against morality per se, as Nagel illustrates above, becomes per force a moral contention, to be evaluated in ethical terms. We cannot step outside morality and remain human.

One might get the impression from the foregoing discussion that the basic problem is that there is a group of materialist villains, or what the British physician-philosopher Raymond Tallis parodies as "neuromaniacs" and "Darwinitics," who in devotion to an ersatz religion of scientism, debunk what is precious, holy, and unique to humanity.[17] Alas, the problem is deeper than that. As the cartoonist Walt Kelly phrased it, we have met the enemy and it is us. We ourselves are constantly guilty of attempting to return our personhood to the world of things. We are so constituted as to allow part of our nature, in Nagel's words, to "escape from the specific contingencies" of the "creaturely point of view."[18] We withdraw into this part—the godlike rationality prized by philosophers such as Plato or Maimonides—allowing it to *detach* from the rest of our personhood. We develop an impersonal conception of the world as well as those parts of ourselves that the rational part finds alien. We have then handed over some significant swath of our being to the world of things.

Nagel sees our situation as one of constantly falling prey to the lure of objectification. Examples include the reduction of persons to selfish genes, love to hormones, actors in a marketplace to the rational choosers of game theory, or autonomy to neural mechanisms. *Whatever truth is to be gained from such objectification is vitiated by the unwarranted presumption of totality and sufficiency that motivates it.* Sellars along with Buber and Heschel would agree. Losing the perspective of the person is a dangerous form of amnesia. Or when deliberate, it is a kind of hubris; it is an overreach typical of scientism, but not of scientism alone. To an extent, the overreach is endemic to rationality as such. Thus, precisely as rational beings we must constantly struggle to reintegrate ourselves and regain the perspective of wholeness, so prized by Buber.

If we fail to reintegrate our third-person view of the world (and ourselves within it) with our first-person perspective, we cannot avoid a massive problem. For "one has to *be* the creature whom one has subjected to detached examination," writes Nagel, "and one has in one's entirety to *live* in the world that has been revealed to an extremely distilled fraction of oneself."[19] But that is well-nigh impossible. Try to substitute "the interpreter module in the left hemisphere is assembling a narrative composed of memories, which are synaptic connections located in the frontal lobes and prefrontal cortex" for "I am thinking about what I enjoyed when I was a child." Or try replacing "neuron 6809D has fired" for "I taste a hint of raspberry in this Bordeaux."[20] In order to do this successfully, one would need to hold to the impersonal viewpoint—Nagel's view from nowhere—*and* accept the immediacy as well as qualitative uniqueness of one's first-person experience. (Why talk about modules or neurons in the first place if there were not an experiencing subject having these memories or tastes?) Perhaps persons with multiple personality disorder could live in such a bifurcated world. Sane persons could not, at least in a single instant. (It could be done sequentially, however. We could, and perhaps should, accept whatever valid deliverances science gives us about ourselves. In a moment of detachment, we could consider the scientific image to explain something critical about *what* we are. But we must then return to *who* we are, reintegrating the new scientific facts with the manifest image of ourselves that we inhabit. We could incorporate the scientific account of what we are, at the level of our nature, into an ever more capacious account of who we are as persons. The error of scientism is its spurning the work of reintegration.)

Scientism's thoroughgoing objectification of human life comes at the cost of the *worth* of persons. At an earlier moment in history, against the background of the scientific revolution of Galileo, Copernicus, and Newton, Kant tried mightily to uphold the worth of persons.[21] Kant is a model, although not an entirely successful one, of the work of reintegration. Struck by the power of scientific explanation and threat a thoroughgoing Newtonian mechanism posed to our self-understanding as persons, Kant asserted a complex human nature. Human beings are citizens of two realms: a phenomenal realm in which we are things among things, and a noumenal or intelligible realm in which we are subjects or persons.

As members of the phenomenal realm we are animals, continuous with the rest of nature, moved by causes (rather than by reasons) and embedded in a mechanistic universe explicable in terms of Newton's laws. As entities continuous with nature, we cannot know or understand what we really are; introspection only reaches so far—it cannot tell me, for example, how my digestion works. Science can take us some way toward unpacking this mystery as, through empirical inquiry, we discover piecemeal how we are fit together, how we work, and *what* we are.[22] But such explanation only reaches so far. This is our story, yet it is not the whole story; if it were, we couldn't tell it. We are also subjects, who look on our objective natural selves at a certain remove. We are persons, not things. We have freedom, we have autonomy, and we have worth.

Why the world allows for such a dimension is unknown. It would have been more parsimonious for the Newtonian, mechanistic, scientific image of the world and man to be exhaustive. But a dichotomized reality, at least at the conceptual level, must be the case in order for what Kant reverently calls "the moral law" to matter. For Kant, nothing matters more than the moral law; the moral law has supreme reality. The "starry heavens above" do not surpass in splendor "the moral law within." Responding through reason and will to the moral law is what makes us human; it grounds our human nature and lifts it above the rest of nature. "Rational beings," Kant writes, "are called *persons* because their nature already marks them out as ends in themselves—that is, as something which ought not to be used merely as a means—and consequently imposes to that extent a limit on all arbitrary treatment of them (and is an object of reverence)."[23] Everything else in nature is a means. Only persons are ends in themselves. The moral law requires that we treat ourselves and all other rational beings never solely as possessing instrumental value, yet always fundamentally as ends, as having inherent value. That some beings should have inherent value is not a "fact of nature" but it is nonetheless a fact. We must integrate the view of ourselves as biological animals, embedded in a causally determined Newtonian universe with a view of ourselves as mysteriously free, rational beings capable of knowing and responding to the moral law, the existence of which is inexplicable in a Newtonian universe.

Kant recognizes, of course, that we often treat others as means. I treat my plumber, for instance, as a highly specific means to unclogging my drain. Kant doesn't mean to override the world of daily interaction; the point is rather to understand that persons are never merely and *solely* means. Precisely by honoring my contract with my plumber, I value his rational nature as a person with who just dealing is imperative. The plumber has entered into a contract with me. In the mutuality of our contract, we recognize and honor one another's standing as persons. We give unspoken testimony to our unimpeachable worth. Furthermore, my own inherent worth as a person generates duties toward myself. The honesty that I am to have toward myself, or duty to develop my talents, follows from Kant's premise of the inherent value of personhood. Kant, controversially, prohibits lying, even the telling of white lies or lies that could save lives, on the basis of my duty to be honest to—to respect the inherent worth of—myself.[24]

In this way, Kant tries to honor both a scientific image of a human being and a manifest one—to be faithful to the science of his day, but also to remain within the traditional orbit of the sanctity or dignity of human life. He gives a secular, post-theological grounding for human worth. He becomes the pre-eminent philosopher of human dignity and human rights. But his argument hangs, as it were, by a hair. It assumes a long Jewish and Christian prologue to the story of human worth, without, of course, invoking that backstory. Yet it is hard to see how Kant's endorsement of human worth, as edifying as it is, escapes circularity. If it does not, as I suspect, then arguments such as Kant's may need help from the very religious sources that they attempt to preempt.

For Kant, a rational being is one who can conceive of a categorical, universal moral law and conform its will to it. Such a being is deserving of respect. Human beings belong, all things considered, to the class of rational beings. (Indeed, they are the only members of the class as far as we presently know. Kant was open to the possibility of extraterrestrial life.) Therefore human beings are deserving of respect. QED. This is a valid deductive argument, but there is no noncircular reason to grant the truth of its major premise—namely, that rational beings deserve respect. Why should such beings be deserving of respect? (Respect means treating a being as an end rather than a means.) Why is a rational being's capacity to follow the moral law more valuable than an elephant's capacity to carry heavy items with its trunk? Why are rational or human capacities thought to be higher than as opposed to simply different from animal capacities? The moral law, conformity with which establishes the warrant for respect, only applies to rational beings in the first place. Isn't the game rigged here in their favor? Kant's privileging of the human (insofar as we are rational) over nonrational beings, his elevation of our status to beings deserving of respect, accords with our normative intuition about ourselves, but doesn't establish it; it assumes it. Absent a prior, prephilosophical conviction that human beings have worth, it is hard to see how a Kantian could rise to a principled respect for them. Some belief in the distinctiveness of human beings and their higher worth must already be in place. It is precisely such beliefs that are suspect, if not disreputable, in some intellectual quarters today.

In my view, stringently secular projects such as Kant's work off the normative capital of generations of biblically informed moral imagination, piety, and commitment. They assume a world in which human beings, their worth and welfare, matter. But their attempts to ground those convictions never quite succeed.[25] They appeal, in an unacknowledged way, to the biblical instincts that motivate them.

To return to Jewish sources is to acknowledge the limits of an Enlightenment project like Kant's. He could assume a millennia-old background of Jewish and Christian teachings about the human in the image of God. We can no longer make that assumption, which means that the insufficiency of Kant's argument on behalf of human worth needs to be buttressed.[26]

For this we must return to the sources, not in defiance or neglect of science and secular philosophy, but in sympathetic yet critical conversation with them.

Toward a Jewish Conception of the Manifest Image

A suggestive attempt by Jewish thought to take the sciences that bear on human nature seriously, and yet assert the radical difference and value of the human, is found in a posthumously published book by a leading modern Orthodox thinker, Rabbi Soloveitchik. In *The Emergence of Ethical Man*, an extended commentary on the first chapters of Genesis, Soloveitchik aimed to construct a philosophical anthropology based on the Bible and drawing on the underlying conceptual assumptions of Jewish religious law (*halakha*).[27]

A striking feature of Soloveitchik's view is the continuity of human beings not only with the animal world but also the plant kingdom. Soloveitchik begins with a naturalistic analysis of plant life emphasizing its independent structure and internal homeostatic balance as well as its dependent, tight integration with its external environment. He shows how the halakha conceptualizes and categorizes organic matter in recognition of these natural traits. In support of Soloveitchik's claim that plants and human beings are analogous, he cites Deuteronomy 20:19, which prohibits the destruction of trees by Israelites when they make war. Trees, being helpless, are not to be destroyed, even though human enemies may be if they refuse to surrender. Plant life as such has ontic worth.

Soloveitchik's overall aim here is to argue that a philosophical anthropology stressing our distance from nature, unnaturalness, and possession of divine, immortal souls is profoundly misguided. The medieval view that treats the natural world as carnal, material, a snare, and a temptation for the divine element within us is, for him, completely wrong:

> Man in the story of creation does not occupy a unique ontic position. He is, rather, a drop of the cosmos that fits into the schemata of naturalness and concreteness. The Torah presents to us a successive order of life-emergence and divides it into three phases; the last of those living structures is man. The viewpoint is very much akin to modern science.[28]

One of the startling consequences of Soloveitchik's harsh indictment of (as he sees it) medieval views is his interpretation of the "image of God" in which we are made. Rather than some transcendent bit of divinity within our corporeal frame, this image is emblematic of God's own "immanence and confinement" in the natural order.[29] Within that order, plant, animal, human, and God are partners.

From here, Soloveitchik goes on to develop a characterization of animal life and then mark off a sphere of human distinction. Unlike plants, animals are dynamic; they move and pursue more complex projects of life. True, much of animal behavior is automatic and instinctual, but animals also learn—an important point that works against the false notion that animals are mere instinct machines.[30] Both animals and humans share these traits; they are driven by biological need to achieve successful patterns of behavior, and then find satisfaction in those behaviors.

Where humans part from other animals is in their awareness of a moral aspect to their instinctual programs, needs, and projects. In classic Jewish fashion, Soloveitchik comes to this point through biblical interpretation. In one verse in Genesis (1:28), God *blesses* the animals: that is, He embeds the animals in their organic form of existence. In the very next verse (1:29), He *speaks* to humans. The difference is significant: "The automatic push and blind, forced movement of *va-yevarekh* [and He blessed] turns into a conscious drive and intelligent movement of *va-yomer* [And He said]."[31] Henceforth, humans become conscious of both their naturalness and natural ability to assess, reflect on, deliberate about, and choose plans of action within the natural order of which they are a part.

Within the Genesis text, the immediate context of "And He said" is God's informing humans what they are allowed to eat. All vegetables and fruits, except for those of the prohibited tree in the Garden of Eden, are open to human beings. Animals, however, are not; Adam and Eve are to be vegetarians. The closeness of humans and animals militates against using the latter for food. Thus, for Soloveitchik, "And He said" entails an ethical dimension. "At this crossroads, animal and man part. The former remains arrested within biological automatism, the latter experiences it on a higher plane—as an ethical opportunity."[32]

In this story of the "emergence of ethical man," the human comes to awareness of freedom, the medium in which ethics becomes possible, only when "man is conscious not only of his oneness with nature, but of his otherness as well." And where does this consciousness come from? Not from some "metaphysical endowment," but instead from the natural ability of human beings to look ahead. The split between humans and nature through directedness toward the future is "the most characteristic mark of human existence."[33]

As in Kant (who hangs in the background of this anthropology through the intermediacy of the Jewish neo-Kantian thinker Hermann Cohen, on whom Soloveitchik wrote his doctoral dissertation), the ethical is set off from the natural. But the dichotomy is much less sharp for Soloveitchik than for Cohen. Yes, human beings rise to an understanding of their own difference from the animal world in an ethical moment. Yet Soloveitchik wants to naturalize ethics. As he develops his view, sin becomes departure from the natural; the eschatological ideal becomes a renaturalization of human action. Of course, nature becomes a highly elastic term. Soloveitchik is writing as a theologian, not as a biologist. What he characterizes as nature would not sustain a disenchanted scientific reading. Nonetheless, the propensity to make the Torah and biology cohere in some sense is significant. Soloveitchik's naturalism is shot through with moments of transcendence; he takes the biblical text as a revealed source of truth, after all. Still, he wants to present us with a view of ourselves, a manifest image that rings true in a scientific age. He is trying to reintegrate a holistic understanding of the human as person with a scientific image of humans as a part of the natural world.

As Soloveitchik's account unfolds, humans become ever more deeply estranged from nature. God's scheme of order is undermined by human overreach in the story of the Fall (to use a Christian term); humans and nature are set at odds. Man's incipient ethical consciousness is thwarted by an aesthetic temptation: the tree was "good for eating and a delight to the eyes" (Gen. 3:6). The motif of pleasure reappears—the satisfaction that comes to animals and humans with the successful consummation of biological drives. Soloveitchik sees the objectification of pleasure for pleasure's sake as a fundamental disruption.

To heal this breach, the Torah is given, reintegrating the aesthetic with the ethical, and the ethical with the natural. The Torah recognizes and respects the biological; it facilitates the hallowing of the organic through the possibility of free human action. Humans are able to rise from animals to "personalities." Their personhood grows in experiences of loneliness, shame, intimacy, and joy—the very point about inwardness and wholeness that Buber makes with reference to Augustine.

Soloveitchik's is a rich and suggestive text, of which I have skimmed only the surface. But this should suffice to illustrate the ambition of a leading modern Jewish thinker to construct a philosophy of human nature broadly compatible with scientific naturalism. Soloveitchik aimed to integrate an ethical and religious image of the human person with a scientific one. It certainly would have been cleaner to go either in the direction of scientism or into dogmatic theology. Yet it would have been false to the real challenges imposed by the intellectual life of our time. Part of Soloveitchik's greatness lies in his struggle, like Maimonides long before him, to live with both the perspective of science and a perspective developed out of the Torah. Jewish philosophy must avoid the easy dichotomies and grapple with both these legacies, for both contain truth. Jewish philosophy (and indeed, Jews; indeed, everyone) should be open to truth whatever its source.

Whatever one may think of his substantive views, Soloveitchik's middle way holds promise. It is a truth-seeking, integrating stance that I will adopt in the next chapter to explore specific Jewish texts on human nature.

Persons in the Image of God

Soloveitchik, quite properly in my view, resisted the idea that what makes humans special is that something divine and immortal, a soul, is joined to what they otherwise share with animals, a body. He sought the distinctiveness of the human not in its radical discontinuity with nature, signaled by the cosmic oddity of a soul, but rather in the responsiveness of the human person, conceived as an integrated whole that has emerged out of a natural matrix, to ethical imperatives. Whole persons, richly endowed with natural capacities, rise to decision, choice, judgment, and action. They take responsibility for their portion of the world. The praxis of moral life, which for Soloveitchik is consummated in the response to divine commands, not a dichotomous soul/body architecture, marks human uniqueness vis-à-vis the rest of nature. The emphasis on the wholeness of personhood as well as its irreducible ethical aspect runs deep in Jewish sources.

Of course, dichotomies are hard to shake. We can't do without them because they are eminently useful. Even if a dichotomy doesn't run all the way down into the furniture of the universe, the contrasts that dichotomies evoke are valuable. I doubt that the dichotomy between "newsworthy" and "not newsworthy" runs deep; it depends on an intersubjective consensus within a given society. Yet it is useful to know what is considered news—and what the news is on a given day—and what is considered trivial, unremarkable, and not worthy of public attention. Dichotomies may be conventional, yet still quite important. Some dichotomies, although expressed in culture-relative language, are likely inevitable. They have depth. They surface in our attempts to talk about our human nature.

Classical Jewish thought assumes and propagates such dichotomies: human beings are bodies and souls, male and female; a little lower than the angels, but not much higher than the animals; descended from a common father and mother, yet divided into nations and races; biologically the same, though unique in their individuality; and a part of nature, yet possessing a power to remake both nature and themselves. What we will see in Jewish thought, I suggest, is an embrace of dichotomies, some familiar from Western thought at large, *and* a strategy to contain them. Soloveitchik is instructive here. He cannot do without a concept of the soul, but he eschews any notion that sets it off, in a ghostly Platonic way, from the body. We can see in Judaism's conceptual creativity an impulse toward parsimony and a reverent naturalism. The sacred is not an ontological add-on to the natural world. It is the capacity of that world, as it has emerged in human beings, to turn toward, to attend to, what is highest.

Underlying the dichotomies is a basic Jewish commitment. Human beings are made in the image of God, and therefore possess intrinsic and undeniable worth. The idea of an image of God, as we will see, has an ethical function. It integrates human nature into personhood and gives persons an ethical orientation. It helps to relativize or even overcome some otherwise-troubling dichotomies such as those, for example, between Israel as the Chosen People and the rest of humanity, or between the damned and the saved. All human beings are created in the *imago dei*, not just the Jews. All who are righteous have a "share in the world to come."[1] The basic Jewish commitment to the worth of all human beings, expressed in the biblical creation stories, incorporates humanity into one original moral community. Its future reconstitution is the hope for the messianic age.

The stories of the creation of the first human pair in the biblical book of Genesis are not mere etiologies, causal accounts of how people got here. They are not competitors with scientific accounts, although some, Jewish and Christian, have taken them that way. Rather, they make up a genealogy in the sense defined by the moral philosopher Bernard Williams: "a narrative that tries to explain a cultural phenomenon by describing a way in which it came about, or could have come about, or might be imagined to have come about."[2] They are stories about values; they both display values and account for them.

The classic instance of such a genealogy is the depiction of the state of nature in the social contract theories of thinkers like Thomas Hobbes, John Locke, and Jean-Jacques Rousseau.

In considering the origins of government, these authors are less concerned with the "real history" of government than with explaining how certain values—rights, equality, authority, obligation, sovereignty, and so forth—might have come into being. So, too, with the narratives that describe the creation and early life of Adam and Eve; they are suggestive accounts, as the great medieval interpreter Rashi (1040–1105) pointed out, of the relation of humans to animals and the rest of nature, the value of humanity, the conflicted nature of human beings, the special place of the Jews in the human family, and so on.[3]

In keeping with this dynamic, the Talmud, too, manifests less interest in creation as fact than in the values that underpin and emerge from the biblical narratives. The Gemara (B. Sanhedrin 38a) observes that "man was created alone" (*y'ḥidi*): that is, in the form of a single person or pair, rather than multiple persons, pairs, or groups. Why? Several answers are offered. Righteous people should not be able to say: our ancestors were righteous and therefore so are we; similarly, wicked people should not be able to blame his or her wickedness on heredity. No one should be excused from his or her own moral obligation. Families have no license to quarrel with other families over whose lineage is superior. Thieves should not think their victims are of a different species from themselves.[4]

The creation stories and rabbinic midrashim that elaborate on them are not derisory flights of pseudoscience. They are essays in core human values—among them, responsibility, respect, and recognition of the individual worth of persons.

Created and Creative Nature

For Judaism, human beings are products of an intentional process: not sports of nature, but creations of God. This likely sets Judaism at odds with those contemporary scientific views that offer a mechanical rather than a purpose-oriented or teleological account of causation. If there is no goal drawing the cosmic process forward—if causation is all push and no pull—then there can be no plan, no design, nothing like an intention guiding cosmogony or evolution. Although I cannot pursue it here, some contemporary scientists and philosophers have sought to bring a sense of purpose or goal directedness back into scientific discourse. Some thinkers see cosmogony and evolution in terms of an ever-increasing emergence of freedom or creativity. Their views are not theistic or Judaic, but they do intuit or insert value into what otherwise might be an entirely meaningless concatenation of causal events.[5]

Although the Bible presents all nature as a product of divine intentionality, human beings are special. According to the midrash (Genesis Rabba 1:14), the creation of heaven and earth on the first day includes the creation of all their denizens. On the subsequent days, individual kinds of creature, both celestial and terrestrial, emerge from the aboriginal creation. Medieval Jewish exegetes perceived in this process an evolution-like development.[6] But human beings were not thought to "evolve" in this way. Rather, they came about through a special act of God. As the Bible famously puts it, "Let us make man in our image, after our likeness" (Gen. 1:26).[7] Precisely to whom or what this "us" refers is not clear—

the midrash and later Jewish thought identify the unnamed others in various ways—but what is unmistakably clear is that God takes a moment for deliberation. He does not just command; He considers. The human being is a product of reflection and choice.

Perhaps we see here, as if in a divine mirror, a reflection of the qualities most constitutive of ourselves. Our relationship with nature is mediated; as much as we are a part of nature, we also stand aside from nature, thinking about it, thinking about ourselves, thinking about ourselves thinking about it. Recursive thought is distinctly human. Students of consciousness call it metacognition. The capacity for reflection and choice is a capacity of our nature that facilitates the emergence of our personhood.

Our heightened capacity for reflection and choice makes us distinct as a class from the other members of the created order. Human uniqueness establishes a dichotomy, but it is not entirely a dichotomy with respect to value. Human beings are at best contingently not categorically superior to other beings. Jewish sources express a remarkable ambivalence about the human, as if to fold humanity back into the world of all the other creatures. If there is something great and godlike about human beings, there is also something pathetic and negligible. The psalmist gives expression to this ambivalence:

When I behold Your heavens, the work of Your fingers,
the moon and stars that You set in place,
what is man that You have been mindful of him,
mortal man that You have taken note of him,

49

that You have made him little less than divine,

and adorned him with glory and majesty;

You have made him master over Your handiwork,

laying the world at his feet,

sheep and oxen, all of them,

and wild beasts, too;

the birds of the heaven, the fish of the sea,

whatever travels the paths of the seas,

O Lord, our Lord, how majestic is Your name throughout

the earth! (Psalm 8:4–10)

Another psalm (90:6) likens humans to grass that withers and dries up at dusk, and yet their Creator has "adorned" them, giving them mastery over His other creatures. Their very existence attests in some way to God's majestic presence throughout the earth. Thus, the human is at once "like a breath; his days are like a passing shadow" (Ps. 144:4) and "little less than divine," imprinted with the image and likeness of God.[8]

Rabbi Akiva used to say, "Beloved is man for he was created in the Image. And even more beloved is he since this was made known to him in the verse, 'For in His image did God make man'" (Gen. 9:6). But as another rabbi, Akavia, used to remind his followers, their origins are "a stinking drop," and their destination is "dust, worms and maggots" (M. Avot 3:1, 3:18). This fundamental dichotomy rings true. We feel ourselves to be utterly insignificant yet valuable in some way— perhaps because, unlike all other insignificant things, we are conscious of our insignificance. We alone, it seems, can take our measure as beings.[9]

In biblical thought, God's greatness is known to the world through the presence of the human, who bears God's image and likeness (*tzelem* and *d'mut*). But what does this actually mean? In the ancient Near Eastern context, image and likeness probably signified something tangible: that humans *physically* resembled God, in whose likeness (d'mut) they are formed (Gen. 1:26). We can infer this from one of the Bible's more startling passages. In a vision of the prophet Ezekiel (1:26), God Himself appears in the likeness of the human (*d'mut k'mar'eh adam*). For at least some of the Bible's priestly authors, then, God and human beings are, as W. Randall Garr writes, "morphologically similar."[10]

The use of cognate terms in Akkadian and Aramaic shows that kings placed images of themselves (*tzalmu*) in temples to their gods. The image both stands for the king and serves a cultic purpose as his surrogate.[11] It becomes part of a ritual drama. It resembles the king physically and hence can also function as his surrogate. The image is part of the person of the king.[12] The term is also used in the ancient Near Eastern setting to refer to the images of the gods, who reside in the temples. The image both represents the god and functions as his embodied presence, accepting sacrificial offerings on the god's behalf.

However repugnant to medieval and modern monotheism, the dual sense of the image of God as *resemblance* and *function* is found in both biblical and rabbinic literature (albeit highly qualified in the latter).[13] A key text, Genesis 5:1–3, has Adam—the image and likeness of God—acting in a god-like manner:

> This is the record of Adam's line. When God created man, He made him in the likeness (*bid'mut*) of God, male and female He created them. And when they were created, He blessed them and called them Man (*adam*). When Adam had lived 130 years, he begot a son in his likeness (*bid'muto*) after his image (*k'tzalmo*), and he named him Seth.

Here, Adam passes on his physical image and likeness to Seth as God had passed on His image and likeness to Adam. But like God, Adam has also become a creator, engendering new life. After the initial creation of humans in the image of God, it becomes the responsibility of human beings to propagate the image, to represent God's glory and majesty; in so doing, humans becomes cocreators with God.[14] Humans function, within their own domain, a bit like God. But what of the more disturbing trope of godlike "physical" resemblance?

Rabbinic literature speculates about the divine image in the physical sense. In Genesis Rabba 8:10, after God creates Adam, the angels chant "holy" before him, confusing him with God. In fact, Adam so resembled God that the angels mistook one for the other. Correlatively, Adam was thought to have initially a luminous and gigantic body; his heel was brighter than the globe of the sun (Leviticus Rabba 20:2; B. Bava Batra 58a). Before his sin, his body was of cosmic proportions (Genesis Rabba 12:6). The point here is not that Adam had a spectacular body similar to the putatively awesome, lu-

minous divine body, but that Adam's body is more than a corporeal entity. Adam contains and produces worlds. The form
that he shares with God, while "physical," is not concrete or
palpable.[15] It is energetic and radiant. In a late midrash (Exodus Rabba 40:3) paraphrased by the scholar Alon Goshen-
Gottstein, "The future generations are all parts of Adam's
body. The body of Adam is actually the great plan for the un-
folding of humanity."[16] If all potential nature lies within
heaven and earth, all potential humanity lies within the body
of Adam. Here the rabbis take the troubling trope of Adam's
physical likeness to God and diffuse it into an ethical insight.
Our species-wide descent from a common ancestor sponsors
our essential moral equality.

This emphasis on the physical image of God comes with an
irony: after Adam's sin, the resemblance is lost. Not only is
Adam's size diminished, but his descendants also become
apelike in appearance (Genesis Rabba 23:6). We become, so
to speak, primates. We become vulnerable to all the evils to
which flesh is heir and then some. For the rabbis, Adam was
once invulnerable to demonic assault. That will only be true
for his descendants if they are immersed in the study of God's
teaching, the distinctive vocation of the Jewish people. The
divine image, in the strictly representational sense, has re-
treated from the world. What is left when "looking like" the
imago dei is no longer possible is *acting* like God, *imitatio dei*.
This implies exercising responsibility, caring for the world.

Thus, the rabbis continue to invoke creation in the image
of God in a functional sense. Imago dei has to do with how we
take responsibility for ourselves and the world. In one famous

aggadah, the sage Hillel tells his disciples that he is going to perform a commandment. When asked which commandment, he replies, "To bathe in the public bath." The disciples question whether this is in fact a mitzvah. Hillel answers, "Yes. If the man appointed to take care of the images of kings, which [the gentiles] set up in their theaters and circuses, scours them and rinses them, and they provide his livelihood, and not only that, but [the attendant] occupies an important place among government officials, then how much more so are we, created in the image and in the likeness of God, commanded [to tend to our own bodies]" (Leviticus Rabba 34:10).[17]

To be created in the image of God means primarily to be required to act in certain ways. Negatively, the sage ben Azzai, who made creation in the image of God *the* great principle of the Torah, said that whoever does not engage in procreative sexual activities "sheds blood" and "annuls the *d'mut*" (Tosefta Yevamot 8:7). Not bringing children into the world, if you are able to do so, diminishes and even annuls the likeness. Procreation is that central, that godly. Procreation—not the biological act per se, but the protracted responsibility of nurturing and raising new life—carries on the work of divine creation. What is also clear here is that the status of the image of God in the world hinges on the action of human beings. If human beings do not take responsibility to perpetuate a godly way of life, God's very presence is diminished or annulled. The Talmud (B. Berakhot 8a) puts it dramatically by saying that the Holy One, blessed be He, has no place in the world other than in the four cubits of the halakha, the divine law as studied and implemented by human beings. Whoever judges truly according to divine law becomes a partner in the creation of the world (B. Shabbat 10a).

Conflicted Nature

God apparently needs human beings to represent Him and carry on His creative work. And yet the creation of humanity is not seen as an unadulterated good. Indeed, the phrase, "And God saw that it was good," which appears repeatedly in Genesis 1, is not applied to the creation of humanity.[18] For its part, the midrash seizes on the pregnant phrase "Let us create man in our image, after our likeness" (Gen. 1:26) to interpolate a fascinating backstory. The "us" in this midrash is identified as God's angelic hosts, who are divided on the question (Genesis Rabba 8:5).[19] Some angels urge, "Let man be created." Others say not.

To the author of this midrash, the angels represent opposing values, illustrated by a verse from Psalms (85:11): "Faithfulness and truth meet; justice and well-being kiss." Here, faithfulness advocates the creation of humans because they will practice faithful loving-kindness; truth cautions that humans will be liars. Justice contends that humans will act justly; peace points to the quarrelsomeness of humans. What then does God do? He seizes truth and throws it to the ground. (Therefore the verse, "It hurled truth to the ground" [Daniel 8:12].) As the angels continue to bicker, He creates human beings.[20]

In a variant of this story in the Talmud (B. Sanhedrin 38b), God also asks the angels for their opinion. When a first group advises against creating human beings, He points a finger at them and they are destroyed in a burst of fire. The action is repeated with a second group of angelic skeptics. The remaining group also leans against, but prudently abstains; God proceeds to create humanity. The subsequent history of humankind, however, leading up to the flood and Tower of Babel, only confirms the angels' suspicions. Afterward, when the angels ask God whether, in retrospect, He made the right decision, He answers obliquely with a verse from Isaiah indicating that He will bear with humanity no matter what.[21] God is forever disappointed by human beings, yet seldom regrets the decision to create them.

Rabbinic ambivalence on this theme does not stem from anxiety about the possible meaninglessness of human life; the sages were not modern existentialists. Their position is better captured in a plaintive prayer of the Siddur:

> What are we? What is our life? What is our faithfulness? What is our righteousness? What is our attainment, our power, our might? What can we say, Lord our God and God of our ancestors? Compared to You, all the powerful are nothing, people of renown as if they did not exist. The wise are as if without wisdom; the understanding as if without reason. Our actions are formless; the days of our lives, ephemeral. The superiority of man over beast is nothing, for everything is futile [*hevel*].

This passage, with its echoes of the biblical book of Ecclesiastes, expresses consternation over the moral weakness of human beings; it does not imply that human existence is purposeless or pointless.[22]

In short, rabbinic ambivalence reflects and reacts to the moral ambiguities of human nature. Although humans bear the image and likeness of God—although they are supposed to play a godlike role in the world—they diminish the image by shunning the role. The students of the early sages Hillel and Shammai argued for two and a half years, so the Talmud tells us, over whether it would have been better had humans not been created. Shammai's students thought yes, it would have been better; Hillel's believed the contrary. Unable to reach agreement, they decided to vote. The vote went Shammai's way, with a qualification: now that humans have been created, let them examine their past ways or, as some would have it, take heed for their future actions (B. Eruvin 13b).

Finally, the midrash portrays God Himself as conflicted about whether He should create humanity. If I do, He reasons, evildoers will arise from Adam; if I don't, there will be no possibility for righteous people to arise. What does God do? Excluding thoughts about human wickedness from His mind, he suppresses His attribute of judgment (*middat ha-din*) and relies on His attribute of compassion (*middat ha-rahamim*) to create humanity (Genesis Rabba 8:4).[23] In other words, He decides to take a chance, hoping that precisely because their nature is conflicted, humans can find within themselves the power to atone for the evil that they will inevitably do and rise to their vocation as God's image in the world. Human nature comes with a built-in propensity for moral failure as well as rectification and rectitude. Our capacity to take stock, change our deep-seated ways, and transcend our given or acquired nature makes us a good gamble, from the Creator's point of view. We may see this, working from the bottom up, as a sign of resolute Jewish hope for human betterment.

Hybrid Nature

What almost prevents God from creating humanity in the first place is humans' potential for evil. Where does this originate? It originates, in part, in the very power to choose. The choice for good, the option to advance the creative work of God in the world, would be meaningless unless we could also choose against it. But what motivates the choice against the good? Part of the problem is that we humans have both an animal and divine nature. It would be easy enough to blame our defection from God's way on our untamed animal nature, but the Judaic account is more complex and subtle than that.

The rabbis differ from Plato (*Phaedrus* 253d–54e), for whom the rational part of the soul has constantly to struggle against the irrational and more animalistic part.[24] In rabbinic Judaism, the latter aspects may be somewhat animal-like, but the tendency toward evil—known in rabbinic literature as *yetzer ha-ra*, the evil impulse or inclination—is itself a divinely created force. God brought it into the world during creation; it enters human beings as they emerge from the womb (Genesis Rabba 34:10), and plays a necessary role in the human drive to survive. As such, according to one midrash, God's statement that His creation was "very good" refers precisely to the evil inclination. Why should the yetzer ha-ra be regarded as very good? For this reason: "If it were not for the *yetzer ha-ra*, no man would build a house or marry a woman or procreate or engage in business" (Genesis Rabba 9:7).[25] The crucial, godlike activity of procreation is traced to the "evil inclination"!

An early story in Genesis—Cain's murder of his brother Abel in a jealous rage—provides a clue as to the paradoxical significance of the yetzer ha-ra. Cain, inventing religion as it were, offers God the "fruit of the soil" as a sacrifice. Abel follows suit by offering "the choicest of the firstlings of his flock." Unaccountably, God rejects Cain's sacrifice and accepts Abel's. Cain sinks into distress and despair—in the biblical idiom, "his face fell" (Gen. 4:5)—so God turns to Cain and counsels him: "Why are you distressed and why is your face fallen? Surely, if you do right, there is uplift. But if you do not do right, sin couches at your door; its urge is toward you, yet you can be its master" (Gen. 4:6–7).

Here we have an early acknowledgment of the near inevitability of moral failure, but also the reparative potential of human decision and resolve. Sin, like an animal, "couches" or crouches—*rovetz*, a word mostly used for animals—at one's door. It is personified; it has an urge (*t'shukah*), a strong desire that will master you unless you master it. All this is somewhat reminiscent of Plato's metaphor of the charioteer struggling to master the horses of eros in *Phaedrus*.[26] In the biblical text, however, the sin seems to have been portrayed as a demon, which the rabbis later identified with the yetzer ha-ra (Genesis Rabba 22:6).[27]

In the biblical story, God reassures Cain that he does indeed have the ability to control this strangely independent, animallike desire (or demon). Even though, as we learn, Cain fails miserably to do so, there is a note here of both realism and hope. Implacable desire, welling up from the depths of our being, may yet be governed if we have the will. (Alternatively, within the context of rabbinic Judaism, the demonic yetzer ha-ra may be fought successfully through the discipline of Torah study.)

The biblical text is not explicit—it is merely suggestive—in linking overwhelming passion to the animal dimension of our hybrid nature. But the midrash develops the suggestion in greater detail. After God says, "Let us make man in our image, after our likeness," He adds, "They shall rule [*yir'du*] the fish of the sea, the birds of the sky, the cattle, the whole earth, and all the creeping things that creep on the earth" (Gen. 1:26). Later, after the creation of humans, God says, "Be fertile and increase, fill the earth and master it; and rule [*r'du*] the fish of the sea, the birds of the sky, and all the living things that creep on the earth" (Gen. 1:28). With its typical attention to small irregularities in the biblical text, the midrash focuses on the difference in grammatical form between the two uses of the verb *r-d-h*, "to rule." Its conclusion: if humans are worthy—that is, if they act as one made in the image of God—then they will rule the animals. If not, they will descend and, diminished in stature, be ruled by them (Genesis Rabba 8:12).[28] Human possibility hangs in the balance. If human beings realize their godlike nature, they shall rule the animals as God rules the cosmos. If human beings fail to realize their nature, they shall fall before the animals, becoming a middling species among them.

The medieval philosopher Joseph Albo (ca. 1380–1444) develops the theme of the relationship between humans and animals in a philosophical sermon on Cain's sin and subsequent fate.[29] His reading also tries to account for God's mysterious favoring of Abel's offering and His spurning of Cain's sacrifice. Albo presents Cain and Abel as representing two different views concerning that relationship. Adam, their father, was not permitted to eat meat despite its health benefits, since the practice of killing animals accustoms people to "cruelty, rage and ... the bad habit of shedding innocent blood." Instead, God assigns to Adam seed-bearing plants as food, while assigning to the animals plants like grass whose seeds are not apparent. The purpose of this was "to show the superiority of the human species to other animals."[30] From observing their father as he cultivates and eats these plants, the two brothers draw different conclusions. Since all eat plants, Cain does not think humans are radically superior to animals. Abel believes that humans have greater relative yet not absolute superiority (insofar as they not only eat plants, like the animals, but *grow* them). Like Cain, therefore, he fails to see the superiority of humans to animals in sufficiently strong terms.

In Albo's reading, God meets Cain halfway. In his consoling address (Gen. 4:6–7), God asks, "Why are you distressed and why is your face fallen?" and asserts, "Surely, if you do right, there is uplift." The meaning of this, Albo claims, is, "You are right: man is born a wild ass and has no superiority over the animal in actuality when he comes into the world, but he has superiority potentially if he practices goodness and realizes his potentialities and recognizes the greatness of the

Lord. If he does well, he will be lifted up above the animals."[31] But Cain listened selectively to God's counsel. He heard that there is no inherent superiority of humans to animals. He thus thought that there was no fundamental difference between his brother and the animals. And since it was clear that God favored Abel's offering over Cain's, he inferred that killing animals was permissible. Hence killing Abel was permissible. Although a wicked passion—envy—enters into Cain's decision, what cinches it is a chain of faulty reasoning. When God comes to punish him, then, Cain does "not yet understand that to shed the blood of a human being is a more serious matter than to shed the blood of an animal."[32]

Albo's reasoning is not entirely clean, bound as it is to a sermonic form and entangled in the interpretation of biblical verses, but his basic claims are apparent enough. There is a radical dichotomy in worth between humans and animals, and to shade this dichotomy is to court conceptual and moral confusion. Nonetheless, it is not an animal aspect of our being that causes us to stray or sin; rather, it is a failure of our uniquely human capacity to reason to appreciate the dignity of the human.[33] He rounds out his sermon by adducing the figure of Seth, Adam's late-born son, who unlike Cain and Abel, but like his father, Adam, is explicitly begotten "in his image, after his likeness" (Gen. 5:3). Albo takes this to mean that Seth recognizes the dignity of the human form that is in the image of God. The image, that is, inheres most fully in those who are self-aware enough to know that they possess it and who act accordingly.

The same conclusion is borne out by the midrashic treatment of Eve and Adam's sin in the Garden of Eden. The serpent, of course, seduces Eve. But why? What is the serpent's motivation? In the view of the midrash, the serpent observed Adam and Eve engaging in sexual intercourse and became jealous. He then wanted to kill Adam so that he could have Eve to himself.[34] His tempting her with the forbidden fruit is quite literally a seduction. Curiously, in this midrash Adam and Eve are not portrayed as somehow imitating the animals in their sexuality; rather, the cleverest animal in the garden wants to imitate *them*. Sexual intercourse is presented as a purely and distinctly human activity, which an animal wants, in a transgressive way, to emulate.

A case could be made that Jewish sources from the Bible through the rabbis of the Talmud all present animals as cognitively diminished versions of human beings versus—as in the modern evolutionary biological perspective—presenting humans as cognitively enhanced versions of animals. In Jewish law, animals are held liable for the damage they cause. The ox in Exodus 21:28 who kills a human is sentenced to capital punishment by stoning—a mode of execution otherwise applied only to humans. The offending ox is not to be slaughtered, nor may its flesh be consumed. It is treated, in a sense, as if it were a reckless, irresponsible human being.

Elaborations of animal liability are found in the Talmud. In one discussion, an ox is held to be so clever that it "intentionally" lights a fire in order to produce ash for medicinal purposes; an ox with a toothache breaks open a keg of beer to the same end (B. Bava Qamma 34a–35b). Thus, we may ascribe to animals some of the morally relevant characteristics of human beings. There is a threshold to such anthropomorphism, however.[35] An ox, for example, may intend to wound a person, but it cannot be thought to intend to shame them. An ox is not conscious of the dignity of the other; it doesn't live in a world in which dignity is a value.

In brief, animals are not viewed as mere brutes or in a monochromatic way. Rabbi Yohanan states that had the Torah not been given, humans could have learned modesty from the cat, honesty from the ant, chastity from the dove, and good sexual manners from the rooster, who endears himself to the hen before mating with her (B. Eruvin 100b). The aspects of our nature that we share with animals are not an alien presence within us. They inform our human nature, but are themselves transformed by it.[36] Humanity is in some ways continuous and in other ways discontinuous with other sentient life. Hence, the cognitive and moral errors that lead to evil choice as well as immoral acts cannot be blamed on our hybrid nature; they are uniquely human failings.

Body and Soul

It would similarly be convenient to ascribe our propensity for virtue to our souls while blaming our penchant for vice on our bodies. There is some of that in Jewish sources, especially those written during the Middle Ages, but the picture is more complicated. The tradition at times asserts a strong body/soul dichotomy and at other times subverts it. The latter move is more compatible with contemporary secular thought. As I mentioned earlier, modern scientific approaches to human nature and our distinctive mental life reject the blatant dualism of much of the philosophical tradition. Dualists like Plato and Descartes are out; monists like David Hume (1711–76) and Benedict de Spinoza are in.[37] For a scientifically minded reader today, reference to the soul may be disconcerting. But let us interpret charitably and try to find what motivates some of the Jewish views, constructing a plausible concept of the soul as we go.

Beginning with figures like Philo in the first century CE, a great deal of dichotomous soul and body talk comes into the Jewish tradition on the wings of Hellenism. But there is an older tradition, found in the Bible, which sees human beings as indissoluble unities, integrated wholes. Subsequent Jewish texts try to hold on to this holistic conception of human nature. The words soul and later self become ways of talking about persons as moral agents oriented to value, responsible to God and others, and identified by their normative commitments.[38]

The key biblical text is Genesis 2:7. "The Lord God formed man from the dust of the earth. He blew into his nostrils the breath of life [*nishmat ḥayim*] and man became a living being [*nefesh ḥayah*]."[39] While in Genesis 1, God creates man and woman together through a speech act ("Let us make man in our image"), in Genesis 2, God creates the male separately by reaching into the soil and forming him out of its clay. Man, *adam* in Hebrew, is shaped from soil, *adama*. (Compare the Latin *homo*, man, and *humus*, soil.)

The guided emergence of the human from the earth is apt. A line earlier, we are told that "there was no man to till the soil." As it would become the man's vocation to keep and tend the garden, cultivate the earth and advance the implicit impulse behind creation, it is fitting for him to be made of the same stuff as his earthly home. The Woodstock generation may have sung that we "are stardust, we are golden, . . . and we've got to get ourselves back to the Garden," but the Bible's view of human origins is somewhat more deflationary. Our origins lie in the dirt. (Yet the elements that make the dirt were formed in the stars; the Woodstock view, notwithstanding its romanticism, has some merit.)

The shaped soil is animated by God's breath. There is no sense in the Bible that this inspiriting force possesses a unique identity or status. God is not breathing into Adam a soul in the Platonic sense of a separable, intelligent entity. Rather, man becomes a living body when the "soil" is vitalized by "breath."[40] Although the animals are not animated by God's breath in any explicit way, they are denominated by the same term, *living being, nefesh ḥayah* (Gen. 2:19), as is Adam. Life, the text implies, forms a single community.[41]

The term nefesh then does not mean soul in a speculative sense; it means living thing. As for the terms *ruaḥ* and *neshama*, they allude to those breathlike forces that energize the nefesh. What is at issue, in other words, is the difference between the living and nonliving; the terms designate that difference without presuming to develop a theoretical account of it. Later, in the Middle Ages, the same words will be pressed into the service of a self-consciously metaphysical outlook, aligned by the medieval philosophers with Aristotle's nutritive, sensitive, and rational dimensions of the soul.[42] But in the Bible, nefesh is not opposed to body. Nefesh integrates breath (ruah, neshama) and flesh (*basar*). Nefesh implies wholeness.

Thus, Psalm 84:3, "my body and soul shout for joy to the living God," speaks of the intense enthusiasm of the whole person for the divine Temple. The famous words of Deuteronomy 6:4–5, which Judaism has taken as a creedal affirmation—"Hear, O Israel! The Lord is our God, the Lord alone. You shall love the Lord your God with all your heart and with all your nefesh and with all your might"—imply the total commitment of one's entire being.[43] In Psalm 78:39, the related term ruah complements basar, flesh. Speaking of God's forbearance in the face of human wickedness, the psalmist writes, "For He remembered that they were but flesh, a passing breath [ruah] that does not return." Flesh and spirit refer to the same being and share the same destiny. Soul is not immortal and body mortal; both are fragile and fleeting, two aspects of an integrated personhood.[44] Indeed, nefesh may be well translated as "person" (as in Lev. 2:1, 4:2, or 7:20)—that is, a responsible being in the eyes of the law.

It is within rabbinic literature that a concept of the soul as a distinct element, separable from the body, begins to surface. When human beings are created, the rabbis imply, God does not simply breathe into them, as He did for Adam; He imparts a pure spiritual substance that it is their responsibility to sustain.[45] If in the Bible we might say that one *is* a soul, in the sense of a whole integrated person, here we might say that one *has* a soul, in the sense of a precious possession.[46]

Two ancient liturgical texts bring out this distinction. The first prayer a Jew says on awakening, Modeh Ani, gives thanks to God for having mercifully "returned my soul to me." My soul is thus a part of me, not (as in the Bible) the whole of me. This is soon followed by a longer prayer drawn from the Talmud: "The soul [neshama] that You, my God, have given me is pure. You created it. You formed it. You breathed it into me. You keep body and soul together. One day You will take my soul from me, to restore it to me in life eternal. So long as this soul is within me, I acknowledge You."[47]

The assertion that the soul is pure (*tehora*) is usually understood to be a rejection of the Christian claim that all souls are corrupted by original sin.[48] The daily return of a pure soul allows one to confront the moral choices and challenges of the hours ahead. The verbs created, formed, and breathed all derive from both the first and second creation stories in Genesis. The allusion to the primordial creation leads to the thought that each day is akin to a new creation, and that, until death, human beings always have another chance. Dread of doom need not weigh on them nor does fate crush them. Creation is not a temporally remote event. It is a trope for moral possibility, a horizon for human action.

The prayer moves from an allusion to creation toward an anticipation of redemption, tying origin to goal, and clearly expressing the intuition of purposiveness that underpins the Judaic account of nature and human nature alike. Although God will one day remove the soul from its fleshy embodiment, He continues to guard the unity of the two and will restore it in the "world to come"—which is to say, at the future resurrection (B. Sanhedrin 90b–91a). In some accounts, the souls of the righteous are stored under the divine throne (B. Shabbat 152b); in others, the soul wanders between the upper world and the body in the grave.

The rabbinic tradition thus seems both to accept the prevailing body/soul dualism of the Hellenistic world and qualify as well as partially subvert it. The soul is not trapped in the body, eager to return to its sublime home in heaven. Embodiment is not a cursed state, and death is not a blessed relief—from sickness, yes; but from life, no. No rabbi talks as Socrates does (*Apology* 40c–42) in welcoming the soul's imminent flight from its corporeal prison. Instead, both soul and body work together to fulfill the human vocation of emulating God in action, and both are jointly necessary conditions for moral life. Moreover—and here is where dualism is not just qualified but also partly subverted—the doctrine of resurrection, which the rabbis locate in the Hebrew Scriptures, guarantees that pure and ethereal as the soul might be, its proper destiny is to be (re)joined to the resurrected body.[49]

This insistence on the corporeal reintegration of the soul was a novelty in antiquity. In the face of their own incipient dualism, the rabbis strain to maintain the Bible's integrated view of human nature.

A final example of this qualified dualism is an aggadah in the Talmud that illustrates the mutual dependence of body and soul, the force of which is to make them jointly responsible for the person they comprise. Antoninus, a philosophical

Roman, challenges Rabbi Judah ha-Nasi with the thought that soul and the body can each free themselves from judgment. The body can plead that it cannot be guilty of sin because as soon as the soul leaves it, it is inert as a stone. Thus, any wrongdoing must be the soul's fault. The soul can plead that once it leaves the body, it flies about like a bird unconnected with the material world in which wrongdoing occurs. They can each blame the other. The rabbi responds with a parable. Consider a king who has a wonderful orchard in which there are delightful figs. He appoints two watchmen, one lame and the other blind, to guard the figs. The lame man is entranced by the figs and tells the blind man how attractive they are. They combine forces, the lame man getting on to the blind man's shoulders and navigating him to the fig trees. When the owner of the garden returns and discovers that his figs have been eaten, he interrogates the two men. The lame man feigns ignorance, saying that he has no feet with which to walk. The blind man makes a similar excuse. The king then resolves to place the lame man on top of the blind one and judge them together. Hence, God at the time of judgment will put the soul back into the body and judge them as a composite whole (B. Sanhedrin 91a–b). The parable accepts the dualistic premise of the Roman philosopher, but negates its normative implication. Body and soul are ordered to moral responsibility; they are axiological, not ontological concepts. From the point of view of moral action and responsibility—which is *the* relevant point of view for the aggadah—the two are aspects of a single moral agent. Agency and responsibility weld the putative constituents of a person into an integrated being.[50]

Although medieval Jewish thinkers go much further than the rabbis in formalizing the dualism of body and soul, they also frequently soften the dichotomy. True, there are genuine Platonists, who see the soul as wholly distinct from the body. But there are eclectic thinkers like Saadya Gaon (892–942) who see the soul as material, albeit formed of fine matter (as opposed to the gross matter of which the body is formed). And there are also Aristotelians, who see the soul as the *form* of the body.[51] What this means, roughly, is that the soul is a capacity, power, or faculty of the body, rather like a skill is to a carpenter.[52] The soul is the naturally organized body's first grade of actuality, of becoming what it inherently, potentially is. The problem of the body/soul dualism does not arise on this account. As Aristotle (*On the Soul* 2:412b6) puts it, "We can wholly dismiss as unnecessary the question whether the soul and the body are one: it is as meaningless as to ask whether the wax and the shape given it by a stamp are one."

All these thinkers, from Philo to Albo, are aware of the scientific discussions among ancient and contemporary philosophers as to the relations between body and soul. They both use and criticize received as well as current views, typically domesticating them to a theological-ethical purpose. Although there is some interest in purely speculative metaphysics, what is at stake for the medieval Jewish philosophers is personhood, the normative dimensions of human nature. Let us consider two arguments, one from the beginning of the medieval philosophical tradition and the other from the end, to illustrate the point.

Is the soul a substance in its own right, or an "accident" or quality of substance? Saadya argues strenuously for the former view and against various versions of the latter. One such version, an influential one, is Aristotle's: the soul is the perfection, as noted above, the "first grade of actuality," of a natural body.[53] The natural body, in order to rise from its potential into actuality, needs to be organized in such a way that it can do what it has the potential to do. "Suppose that an eye were an animal," Aristotle (*On the Soul* 2:412b 20) writes, then "sight would have been its soul." An eye has the potential to see; sight constitutes its actuality. Put a little differently, the soul is that which allows the eye to achieve its function. It is not some separate substance but instead the means by which a natural entity fully functions within the bounds of nature and realizes its distinctive purpose.[54]

Saadya rejects this notion and all others that deprive the soul of substantive status. He believes that in order to support the qualities that we ascribe to it, the soul cannot itself be a quality or, more comprehensively, an accident, since "the soul is affected by many accidents."[55] It therefore must be a substance. But what kind of substance? "The quality of the soul is that of a pure substance similar to the substance of the celestial spheres."[56] Indeed, the soul is of a more refined substance than the spheres, since the spheres do not have intellect while the soul is endowed with reason. And yet the soul can act only through the body; only when body and soul are combined can the faculties of appetite (nefesh), passion (ruah), and knowledge (neshama) become manifest.

Given Saadya's (modified) form of dualism, why does he not follow Plato in seeing the conjunction of soul and body as a calamity for the soul? Here, the moral faith of Judaism impedes his Platonism. He faces the problem head-on:

> I found people who argued thus: "How can we reconcile the wisdom of the Creator (be He exalted and glorified) with the fact that He placed this noble soul, which is purer than the sphere, within this ignoble bodily frame?" They were inclined to believe in their hearts that God had inflicted evil upon the soul. . . .
>
> My view is that the soul by itself is, on account of its nature, incapable of action, and that, for this reason, it was necessary to join it to something through which it became capable of virtuous activities so as to attain by such activities eternal bliss and perfect happiness.[57]

In brief, the soul may be pure, but it's unfinished; it needs the challenges and opportunities of life in the world to reach its full stature. If it lives wisely, righteously, and well, its matter will become even more luminous and refined. If its embodied life is morally impoverished, it will coarsen. In life, refinement is always possible through repentance, but after death the die is cast. Agency departs along with embodiment.

So why did God not spare us all this and simply leave the soul free of a bodily condition? The answer is that the highest good is obedience to God, and obedience is only possible within the contours of worldly existence. To think about the soul in isolation from that context "is tantamount to asking that the soul should not be a soul."[58] Besides, "there is nothing impure about the human body; on the contrary, it is perfectly pure."[59]

Saadya thus asserts a soul/body dualism, but like his rabbinic predecessors, qualifies it and puts it at the service of a normative agenda. He radically affirms the goods of this world; the soul is made for the body, so that the two of them may strive to live in obedience to and in imitation of God. The soul is separable from and outlives the body, such that at the end of days, it can be reunited with it, and judged by God and given reward—or punishment—for its actions. The metaphysical story serves to uphold a belief in the ultimate reality of justice.

At the end of the medieval Jewish philosophical tradition, the same pattern is visible in Albo, whose way of distinguishing between humans and animals was considered earlier in this chapter.

What motivates Albo's treatment of the soul is the fourfold question of whether human beings are rewarded and punished wholly in this world, wholly in the world to come, in both, or (most heretically) in neither. This is the framework within which he develops his doctrine of the soul—even as he is quick to point out that the Torah itself enjoins moral-halakhic behavior for its own sake and not for the sake of receiving a reward.[60]

Albo's fourfold question correlates with four views about the nature of the soul. The first one, reminiscent of Cain's in Genesis, is that human souls are not different in kind from the souls of animals. This basic likeness implies that God has no greater concern for humans than for other creatures. Given this, there is no reward and punishment for human beings any more than for other animals, either in this world or the world to come.

Except for the lingering aroma of theism, this thoroughly reductionist naturalism would be congenial, one imagines, to the outlook of scientistic debunkers of religion. Needless to say, Albo will have none of it. The philosophers, he claims, have already refuted it with the argument that human souls have the capacity to conceive universals whereas animals can conceive only particulars; that humans, unlike animals, can continue to think about things when they are no longer physically present to sense them; and that humans, again unlike animals, can engage in analysis and distinguish substance from accident. It follows that the human soul must have some special purpose available to it, some perfection that is unavailable to animal souls. By implication, the human soul is therefore a unique object of divine concern.

The second view is that reward and punishment are meted out only in this world, and this is because the human soul, although superior to those of animals, is also mortal, disappearing on the death of the embodied person. Just as nutrition and perception cease when the soul-body organism breaks down and dies, so too will intellection (the distinctive activity of the rational, nonanimal dimension of the soul).

Albo rejects this, too. Some aspects of the soul, like growth, cease after the age of forty; not so with intellection, which in fact grows more powerful as other human faculties decline with age. The rational dimension of the soul, being different in kind from its other faculties, does not share their fate and does not perish along with the body. Thus, reward and punishment are not limited to this world.

The third view, shared by some great rabbis, including Maimonides, is that reward or punishment is apportioned in the world to come; it is futile to expect justice in this vale of tears, where outcomes are not scaled to moral virtue. A Talmudic aggadah (B. Kiddushin 39b), which narrates the tragic death of a child in pursuit of a mitzvah at his father's behest, shows the futility of expecting justice in this world. Only when the soul is no longer tied to the body can it reach perfection and achieve its just deserts through permanent union with the divine intellect (or in Aristotelian parlance, the active intellect).

Albo's retort takes issue with the version of human perfection that underpins this otherworldly view.[61] If Maimonides and others are correct that "salvation" consists in a union of one's rational soul with the divine intellect, few will ever reach such an end. How could that be just? How could it be God's plan? Albo favors the approach of his teacher Hasdai Crescas (d. 1412): the highest human end is not the abstract intellectual apprehension of God but rather the love of God.

Accordingly, the fourth perspective—that reward and punishment are apportioned both in this world and the world to come—is the one that Albo thinks best characterizes Judaism and is most correct. It is supported by a kind of body/soul dualism that sees both components as necessary to serve God. In this conception, what is distinctive about the human soul is its capacity not for pure intellection but rather the loving service of God. Human intellectual understanding, then, is ordered to a normative moral end. Epistemology serves ethics; logic serves love.

In arguing his point, Albo recalls the tradition's teachings about schoolchildren. As soon as children are able to respond "amen" to a blessing, they begin to share in the life of the world to come. The Talmud teaches (B. Shabbat 119b) that the breath of schoolchildren sustains the world. If so, Rav Papa asked Abaye, What about your breath and mine? Abaye answered that there is no comparing the breath of innocent children and that of adults, with its admixture of sin. Albo concludes from this story:

> Now if the soul is not an independent substance, how can school children, who have attained a very small degree of cognition, be superior to Abaye and Raba who attained a very high degree, without doubt?
>
> The truth is that a very small degree in God's service on the part of one who is not stained by sin avails more than a high degree of one who is stained by sin; for the soul, being an independent spiritual substance, depends for its degree of worth upon the measure of its purity and its worship of God by fulfilling the commandments.[62]

For medieval Judaism, whatever other part might be played by talk about the soul, the role of providing a conceptual framework for agency and responsibility is crucial.[63] Despite the dualistic metaphysics that the medieval philosophers inherited and absorbed, the bent of their work is to remain true to the biblical vision of a moral universe anchored in persons, responsibility, and character.

Self and Other

Talk of the soul is one way, an old way, of thinking about what integrates our sentient and sapient, animal and human dimensions. It is also a way of speaking about what is highest in us, what we hope is most permanent and enduring. The concept of the soul addresses such questions as: What are we really? Is there, at bottom, a single center of consciousness, experience, decision, judgment, and memory—or are we simply the sum of the mental activities that are happening here and now? And what unifies us over time, allowing the adult of today to recognize oneself in the child of yesteryear? Is there a basis for my sense of internal unity; is there an I, and, if so, what is it? Is it a kind of thing, a substance or entity, or a kind of process, activity, perspective, or stance?

For much of Western and Jewish history, the concept of the soul provided the context within which these questions were raised and answered. Today, we are likely to speak less of the soul and more of the self. But that term is hardly less problematic than its predecessor.

Selfhood is not a fixed quantity; it does not designate an object, like *pancreas*. It has no ostensive definition; you cannot point to it. Instead, the term captures whatever concept of personhood prevails in a given society at a given time, and that concept will at least partly comprise moral values. The question of my identity is always in part a question of what I stand for. "We are only selves insofar as we move in a certain space of questions, as we seek and find an orientation to the good," philosopher Charles Taylor writes.[64] Thus, a Homeric self may differ from a Hebraic self, a self within a hierarchy motivated by martial values may differ profoundly from a self in a society shaped by Romantic notions of individuality and expressiveness. A self in a traditional Confucian family differs from a self in an atomized postmodern world, and so forth.

These distinctions go extremely far down. They are not varying interpretations of a given entity; the "entity" itself is up for grabs.[65] Selfhood is what it is experienced to be. But how we think about our experience also conditions that experience. A positive feedback loop is at work. Our experience of life as persons, agents, and conscious selves is shaped by our concepts of our role, place, value, orientation, and end. (All these are culture bound, although not necessarily culture relative. We can, after all, make sense of what it was to be a person in ancient cultures as well as in differing modern ones. Crosscultural understanding weakens the case for relativism.) Our nature imposes physical, chemical, and innumerable biological constraints on us. Yet our cultures build on those constraints, coevolve with them, and shape disparate ways of being a person.[66]

In the traditional Jewish context, the self is not thought of as atomistic, autonomous, or sovereign. Rather, the self is constituted by its *relations* with others and God. "Either social intercourse [*ḥevruta*] or death [*mituta*]," the Talmud says (B. Taanit 23a). (I remarked above that Buber thought Augustine, in gaining awareness of the inwardness of human consciousness, was an advance over Aristotle yet still a less than adequate approach to wholeness. This is what Buber meant: the wholeness of the person is constituted fully in relation with others.) Taylor's characterization of selfhood applies well to classical Judaism: "One is a self only among other selves. A self can never be described without reference to those who surround it."[67] On Taylor's account, the self is formed within "webs of interlocution"—that is, within the skein of questions that we ask ourselves, and that are asked by others about who we are and what we stand for.[68] "Am I my brother's keeper?" Cain's question may have been cynical and disingenuous, or naive and searching, but it was assuredly the right *kind* of question. Cain sought a basis for his selfhood; what kind of being should he be?[69]

Genesis 2 offers an early glimpse of selfhood in the context of relation. Unlike the account of creation in Genesis 1, in Genesis 2 man is created singly and prior to the creation of the beasts. After forming him from the dust of the earth, God places him in the garden "to till it and tend it" (Gen. 2:15). Already, man's relation to his origins in the soil defines him; he is placed in a position of responsibility toward the earth, and his potential for action (cultivation of the garden) acquires orientation, purpose, and limits (not eating the fruit of the tree of the knowledge of good and evil). Whereas in Genesis, chapter 1, the human pair was given a task relative to their own inherent biological nature (be fruitful and multiply), here a relation with another, the earth, is enjoined. For Genesis 2, which is usually thought to be both literally and metaphorically an "earthier" story, the definition of man is intrinsically relational.

God recognizes the relational nature of the being that He has created: "It is not good for man to be alone. I will make a fitting helper for him" (Gen. 2:18). Man needs companionship. God creates the many kinds of land animals and birds, and man enters into a limited form of relationship with them by naming them—an exercise in which God defers to man as to a cocreator: "Whatever the man called each living creature, that would be its name" (Gen. 2:19). Yet none of these creatures satisfies his deep longing for sociality, for the kind of complementarity requisite to his nature. So God causes him to fall into a deep sleep, and from Adam's rib fashions a woman. Adam awakes in a shock of joyous recognition: "This one at last is bone of my bones and flesh of my flesh. This one shall be called woman (*isha*) for from man (*ish*) was she taken" (Gen. 2:23).

And this, the text adds, is why "a man leaves his father and mother and clings to his wife, so that they become one flesh" (Gen. 2:24). Becoming "one flesh" is a good that is relatively independent of the good of procreation ("be fruitful and multiply") in Genesis 1.[70] The deep complementarity found in sexual love has value above and beyond its service to the production of offspring. Bonding is as important as procreation. Hence, in Judaism, a man is commanded not only to procreate but also to provide his wife with sexual pleasure. Sexual activity is to continue after the years of procreation have passed.

The midrash, no doubt affected by the Greek motif of the primordial androgynous being who we meet in Plato's *Sympo-*

sium, provides a context for the complementarity of man and woman: "Rabbi Yirmiyah ben Elazar said: When God created Adam, He created him androgynous, as it is written: 'male and female created He them.' Rabbi Shmuel bar Nahman said: When God created Adam, He created him double-faced, and sawed him [in two], giving him two backs, one back facing one direction and one back facing the other" (Genesis Rabba 8:1).[71]

On one level, the midrash is attempting to reconcile the two creation accounts. In the Genesis 1 version, man and woman are apparently created in a single stroke: "In the image of God He created him; male and female He created them" (Gen. 1:27). In the second story, man is created first and then woman is extracted from him. The midrash implicitly fuses the two stories. God created man and woman together, as an androgynous being, and then separated the two.

But the midrash is also doing something more than textual harmonization. It is giving an account of the moral significance of sexual distinction. Adam and Eve are coeval in the sense that they cannot fully be themselves without each other. They are alike and different. Eve is bone of Adam's bone and flesh of his flesh, yet she is her own person. Adam recognizes both her independent standing and profound relatedness to him. The midrash dramatizes this sameness and difference in a mythical mode: the two were one until God "sawed" them in half. The rabbis give the motif a terse formulation: no man without a woman; no woman without a man; neither one without the *sh'khina*, the presence of God (Genesis Rabba 22:2).[72] The point is probably that neither man nor woman can bring forth new life without the other, nor can both complete the process without divine assistance. Still, the dictum serves equally well as an expression of the complementarity and relatedness that obtain regardless of procreative outcomes. Male and female selves are dependent variables.

The biblical and rabbinic approaches envision an embodied, gendered, relational selfhood in a purely heterosexual mode. It is interesting that Plato's genealogical myth considers homosexual and heterosexual companionship to be equally primordial. In the *Symposium* (189d), Plato relates that in the beginning, human beings were divided into three categories: men, women, and the androgynous beings. The last-named beings were strong and menacing, and Zeus worried about how to control and diminish them without destroying them. Slicing them down the middle and performing some plastic surgery on the resulting halves did the trick. The survivors of these primordial hermaphrodites wanted nothing more than to reunite (191a), and are represented today by men who crave the company of women, and vice versa. As for the descendants of the primordial nonandrogynous males and females, these crave members of their own sex. Among the males, "they have no natural inclination to marry and beget children. Indeed, they do so only in deference to the usage of society, for they would just as soon renounce marriage altogether and spend their lives with one another" (192b). The deep companionship that such men and women find with their own kind includes erotic pleasure, but goes far beyond it. Their complementarity is so deep as to elude easy articulation or explication (192c).

Plato thus gives a mythical foundation for same-sex as well as male-female bonding. The rabbis are no less forthright in offering a genealogical basis for the human need of companionship, but for them homosexuality is disallowed. It is not an equally warranted expression of human nature or enactment of human selfhood. It is considered a kind of moral error, an occasion of succumbing to an errant desire. In Jewish law, both in the Bible and subsequent rabbinic legislation, certain sexual activities between men (but not between women) incur the death penalty.

Needless to say, these sources and the cultural attitudes they have helped to shape have caused enormous pain as well as consternation to gays, lesbians, and others along with their allies. They have been subject to harsh criticism today. The claim now made is that sexual orientation, in its diversity, is natural, innate, and perhaps genetically determined or predisposed.[73] If this is true, human nature may give rise to sexual diversity in the way envisaged by Plato, but not by the biblical and rabbinic texts. It can also be said that in a modern society, an attitude shaped by Greek sources on this question would facilitate greater sexual liberty than an attitude shaped by biblical and rabbinic ones. Whether that would lead to human flourishing in the Judaic (or Christian) manner is another question entirely.

Complementarity is no idyll. Their praise of marriage notwithstanding, the rabbis recognize the pitfalls of relatedness. Commenting on the peculiar biblical phrase *ezer k'negdo*, a fitting helper (traditionally, "a helpmeet for him"), they say that if a man is worthy, his wife will be a help (*ezer*) to him; if unworthy, she will be against him (*negdo*) (B. Yevamot 63a). The opposition of self and other can be positive or negative; it depends on the moral status of the persons so related. (In this Talmudic text, everything turns on the moral character of the husband.)

Negative opposition is itself an all too familiar way of being, again starting in Genesis. Indeed, violence is as old as bonding. The Bible equates murder with fratricide. In Genesis 4, where Cain slays Abel, the brothers come from the same womb, shaped at the same time by the same man, woman, and God. What went wrong? Within the framework of the story, as we saw earlier, Cain sets out for mysterious reasons to please God through offering a sacrifice, but his high hopes are dashed when the sacrifice is rejected and he feels the pain of repudiation. He fears failure, loss, and perhaps his own volatile emotions. God's words of comfort fail to quiet him. He broods on his pain, nursing anger toward God, himself, or Abel, and finally schemes to waylay his brother. Ever the farmer, he sows the ground with Abel's blood.

The text is spare on the subject of Cain's feelings, thoughts, and motivations (as it generally is on the psychological dimensions of its characters), but one thing is clear: he does not react as an animal does, in a patterned response of aggression. Cain comes to his violence in a human way, through conflicting feelings, confused appraisals, and failures of rationality and restraint. He forgets that his brother is like himself. He enters a cognitive blind spot, where knowledge of good and evil—the very knowledge that his parents acquired at high cost—fails him. He "founds" murder, just as he later founds the first city.

From Cain onward, aggression becomes a cultural artifact. The capacity for violence, for fully orchestrated war making, clearly has roots going back to our mammalian ancestors, but its instantiation in human affairs is connected with the evolution of culture. As Wilson writes,

> Although the evidence suggests that the biological nature of humankind launched the evolution of organized aggression and roughly directed its early history across many societies, the eventual outcome of that evolution will be determined by cultural processes brought increasingly under the control of rational thought. The practice of war is a straightforward example of a hypertrophied biological predisposition. Primitive men cleaved their universe into friends and enemies and responded with quick, deep emotion to even the mildest threats emanating from outside the arbitrary boundary. With the rise of chiefdoms and states, this tendency became institutionalized, war was adopted as an instrument of policy of some of the new societies, and those that employed it best became—tragically—the most successful. The evolution of warfare was an autocatalytic reaction that could not be halted by any people, because to attempt to reverse the process unilaterally was to fall victim. A new mode of natural selection was operating at the level of entire societies.[74]

Our peaceful ancestors, like Abel, were reduced or destroyed. The warlike hominids, the sons of Cain, built cities and henceforth civilizations.

The cultural coevolution of aggression can be seen in the odd story of Lamech, a fifth-generation descendant of Cain. A brief, probably fragmentary poem records his strange, boastful homage to his ancestor:

> And Lamech said to his wives,
> "Adah and Zillah, hear my voice;
> O wives of Lamech, give ear to my speech.
> I have slain a man for wounding me,
> And a lad for bruising me.
> If Cain is avenged sevenfold,
> Then Lamech seventy-sevenfold." (Gen. 4:23–24)

Lamech is apparently bragging about taking vengeance on another man and a boy. He mimics Cain, but without Cain's possible excuse of ignorance—or God's extension of the possibility of grace. Here, violence is intentional, disproportionate, and wanton. It is the subject of song. Lamech has arrogated to himself the role of divine protector and judge, all vengeance and no grace. He lives by a code of unbounded vendetta.[75]

The verses that precede the poem tell of the invention of "lyre and pipe" along with "implements of copper and iron." Such technological advance is made possible by the city, founded by Cain, but so too is Wilson's "autocatalytic" violence: an endless negative feedback loop of action and reaction, wounding, bruising, and slaying. The poem is followed by news of a fresh beginning ("Adam knew his wife again and she bore a son and named him Seth" [Gen. 4:25]), passing silent judgment on the human failure of Cain's progeny. A new line, once again created in the image of God (Gen. 5:3), takes the stage.

If the Bible is done with Cain the progenitor of violence, the midrash is not; it gives Cain a second chance. According to the midrash, no one taught Cain that murder is wrong, nor was he aware that hitting his brother with a rock could kill him. He is guilty of, so to speak, involuntary manslaughter rather than first-degree murder, which is why his punishment is exile and not death (Genesis Rabba 22:12). Moreover, Cain responds to divine justice and mercy; fully realizing what he has done, he now repents of his action. As he goes forth into exile, he meets his father, Adam, who asks what his punishment is. Cain responds that God has given him clemency. Adam strikes himself in astonishment at the power of repentance (Genesis Rabba 22:13).

Here, the sinful son teaches the father a moral lesson, ironically succeeding where the father had failed. Adam may have gained knowledge of good and evil, but it seems to have been an abstract kind of knowledge, needing time and choice, exempla and exemplars, to develop into moral knowledge. Adam learns from Cain what evil is and how its grip may be loosened. Cain becomes an example of the penitent, through which the rabbis express their faith that violence—even in the person of the perpetrator—is not ultimate. It is part of our nature, but so too are remorse, repentance, the resolve to reestablish bonds, and the acceptance of punishment for harm done. Cain cannot repair the harm done to Abel, yet he can move forward, chastened and reformed. Without the possibility of moral rejuvenation, the project of selfhood fails. *Teshuvah*, repentance, reintegrates and renews the self.

Vulnerability, Mortality, and Eternity

No one who lives a human life can be unaware of how much we depend on each other, the constant possibility of physical and mental suffering, or the prospect of our certain demise. The anthropologist Melvin Konner reminds us that Hobbes's famous portrayal of a state of nature where everyone is independent of everyone else is a biological impossibility.[76] The reality is otherwise; we are hardwired for cooperation. Without ramified webs of mutual dependence, none of us would exist.

Yet we are also prone to denying this reality. We are "dependent, rational animals," in Alasdair MacIntyre's apt juxtaposition—but in the Western tradition, the rational has often pulled against the dependent.[77] Our capacity for rationality, the transient achievement of a "view from nowhere," has sometimes beguiled us into thinking that we are most essentially detached and independent minds. Franz Rosenzweig thought that the valorization of isolation in the name of metaphysical clarity was the essence of paganism.[78]

Aristotle comes close to embracing such a nondependent version of personhood near the end of his *Nicomachean Ethics*. We are at our most human, he suggests, when we are at our most godlike—that is, when we are engaged in pure, solitary contemplation; this, in Aristotle's view, is God's own activity. But he also acknowledges the concessions that must be made to the human condition. "Being a man, one will also need external prosperity; for our nature is not self-sufficient for the purpose of contemplation, but our body also must be healthy and must have food and other attention" (*Ethics* 10:8). Plato was driven back to the cave, and Aristotle back to the city. The highest intrinsic value, the contemplative life, must be secured by recourse to lower values.

On this account, the dependent self is an inferior aspect of an autonomous self. Vulnerability is our lot, but our true, rational self soars above our corporeal condition on wings of pure thought.

The Jewish tradition has rarely taken such a transcendent turn. Instead, we are at our best, we are most like God, when we walk in His ways. This is a matter of right thought *and* right action. Even Maimonides, who comes the closest to a purely intellectualist thesis, struggles to reconcile the transcendent, Aristotelian self with the relational, rational, but dependent self of his rabbinic lineage.

In the first chapter of his *Guide of the Perplexed*, Maimonides forcefully asserts his basic claim: the Torah's teaching that humans are made in the image and likeness of God does not mean that God has a perceptible form but instead that humans have intellect, or "intellectual apprehension": a godlike quality that does not depend on the physical in any way.[79] What for Maimonides is most valuable, distinctive, and constitutive of human beings—namely, mind at its highest realization—is entirely independent of their embodiment in the physical world or reliance on one another.

At the end of the *Guide*, Maimonides speaks of the telos, the perfection, of human life.[80] What should we strive for, given the kind of being that we most essentially are? Most people get this wrong because they see human beings primarily in their corporeality and sociality. They fail to see what human beings essentially are. They thereby mistake instrumental values for inherent ones, foolishly substituting subservient goods for the true good. Consequently, they lose sight of our ultimate perfection.

There are, says Maimonides, four candidates for this ultimate perfection: perfection of possessions, body, moral virtue, and intellect. He makes short work of the first two: amassing great wealth, and focusing on physique, health, strength, and beauty. Neither of these can be said to belong to what is distinctively and constitutively human in us. Even the third, the perfection of moral virtues, fails the test of self-sufficiency. Moral virtues facilitate social life, but they do not perfect the individual in anything; for the individual needs them and they become useful to only in regard to someone else.[81]

On this last point Maimonides sets himself up for a clash with rabbinic tradition. He claims that most of the commandments serve no other end than the achievement of moral perfection—and yet since moral perfection requires society as its medium, it is not self-sufficient. Only the knowledge of the ultimate principles of reality, the fulfillment of the intellect that is in the image and likeness of God, constitutes true human perfection. And the medium of that perfection is the purely contemplative life. Everything else is either irrelevant or preparatory.

But then Maimonides does something similar to Aristotle, his master and model: he pulls back from this highly intellectualist account of the goal of human life to restore a moral and political dimension. Unlike Aristotle, however, he does this not as a concession to human weakness but instead in the name of imitatio dei. When all is said and done, we are most like God when we walk in His ways, doing His will in our conduct with our fellows. The active and not the contemplative life is the highest service of God, or rather, ultimately the two are mutually supporting. To achieve intellectual apprehension of God, it is necessary to emulate His attributes of lovingkindness, judgment, and righteousness.[82] When Moses asks God to reveal His presence (*kavod*) to him (Exodus 33:18), God reveals His goodness (*tuvi*) (Exodus 33:19). To know God is to know which values are ultimate.

Maimonides has thus regained a conception of human nature more compatible with prior Jewish thought than his Hellenic inspiration might otherwise have allowed. But he still pays a price. In the end, human nature is not characterized by embodiment, vulnerability, dependence, and sociality. We are, at our most inward and essential, purely rational beings who can gaze toward the ultimate even though we return to our fellows and act graciously toward them so that we can act as God acts. Maimonidean humans shun the solitary, contemplative life and turn to the city as the context in which they should seek their perfection. Like the philosopher king, they return to the cave. But like the philosopher king, they retain an awareness of their radical difference from the "vulgar," the mob, which inhabit the cave. One does not get the sense that the intimate particularity of life with people matters much for Maimonides. All of it needs to be regulated by law, the ultimate aim of which is to train us to leave the world thereby regulated. Maimonidean humans do not want to linger on the particular out of love for the world. His is a severely intellectualist vision of the self and its ends. Rationality pulls us away from mutuality; the self at its transcendent height knows nothing of vulnerability and dependence.

For Maimonides, suffering—perhaps the fullest expression of our vulnerability as embodied beings—comes about because we lose our connection to transcendent reality. He sees in the story of Job, a righteous man whose suffering occurs without reference to moral desert, a parable on the failure of wisdom. Job as Maimonides views him was a righteous man, but not a *wise* one. He knew God only through tradition and authority, not through independent, rational speculation and apprehension. Job's misfortune and bitter accusations against God endure only so long as this apprehension eludes him. "But when he knew God with a certain knowledge, he admitted that true happiness, which is the knowledge of the deity, is guaranteed to all who know Him and that a human being cannot be troubled in it by any of all the misfortunes in question" (*Guide* 3:23). At the end, Job confesses that he had spoken against God "without understanding"; he recants and relents, admitting that he is but dust and ashes.

Maimonides takes this to be a disclosure of Job's newfound intellectual insight into the divine governance of the world.

When intellect grasps the ultimate, the misfortunes of life are as nothing. As in Greek Stoicism, where the achievement of a metaphysical vantage point allows the sufferer to transcend their suffering and see once-cherished goods as matters of relative indifference, so here an exalted intellectual perspective minimizes and eliminates suffering. What once mattered need not matter anymore. One retreats to a bastion of transcendent security.

This is perhaps a constant temptation or possibility for religion. It is a glorious thing to believe that the Lord prepares a table for me in the presence of my enemies, and that though I walk through the valley of the shadow of death, I need fear no evil, accepting the grievous misfortunes of life as God's will, and certain that I am ultimately loved, affirmed, and protected. But do such thoughts mark the attainment of an inexhaustible strength, resolve, and orientation, or do they indicate a loss of reality, a break with the world we share? Do they represent the crown of religious faith or its discrediting?

A nonphilosophical engagement with this problem may be found in the Talmud. In struggling to make sense of suffering, the Talmud weighs how much credence to give to explanations that depreciate and depersonalize the experience. The standard model is that of reward and punishment. If one suffers, it is because one has sinned. Yet this straightforward formulation is what comes under challenge in the book of Job, and the rabbis cannot simply let it stand.

The Talmud (B. Berakhot 5a) comments on a disturbing verse from Isaiah ("But the LORD chose to crush him by disease ... that through him the LORD's purpose may prosper"

[Isaiah 53:10]), which maintains that God afflicts those with whom He is *pleased*. If one is suffering and unable to ascribe the cause to transgression, then one should ascribe it to a failure to study Torah. But if one has been studying Torah, then one should understand the condition as the "sufferings of love," imposed by God in order to give a righteous person further opportunity to accrue merit. Sufferings of love are not punishment. If anything, they attest to one's virtue. "For whom the Lord loves, He rebukes as a father the son whom he favors" (Proverbs 3:12). If one acquits oneself well—as Abraham did in his ultimate trial, the binding of Isaac—then he will see his children prosper in the course of a long life; his Torah learning will endure. In order for sufferings of love to fulfill their purpose, though, they must be interpreted by the sufferer as coming from God for one's own good—that is, through the lens of a theodicy.

Theodicy—the defense of God's goodness despite the existence of evil—is the stock in trade of all religious thought. What follows in the sequel is remarkable, however. The Talmud adduces three brief stories of pious rabbis who suffer, but refuse to accept the redemptive significance of their suffering. Indeed, they and their friends accept "neither the sufferings nor their reward."

In the first two instances, a friend of the sufferer extends his hand and lifts the suffering rabbi to his feet. We are not told the meaning of this simple gesture of love, kindness, and solidarity, but it appears to be what is left after metaphysical interpretations are declined. In the final story, the suffering Rabbi Eliezer sits in the dark, bares his arm, from which light emanates, and weeps. His friend, Rabbi Yohanan, asks him why he is weeping, and tries to comfort him with the thought that the problem might be insufficient Torah study, poverty, or lack of children. Yet Rabbi Eliezer responds that he weeps "on account of this beauty that is going to rot in the earth" (B. Berakhot 5b). Rabbi Yohanan agrees that one *should* weep for the loss of such beauty, sits down and weeps alongside, and ultimately raises Rabbi Eliezer by joining him in declining both "the sufferings and their reward."

These are provocative and perplexing stories. Are we to conclude from them that the rabbis don't believe their own traditions about resurrection or life in the world to come? Hardly. But they do seem to allow themselves a Job-like moment, giving its due to the enormity of suffering as experienced from an intimate, first-person point of view, and suspending religious metaphysics in favor of love, friendship, and mutual dependence. Vulnerability is not an illusion and not our fault; it is our lot, before which our most earnest theodicy must sometimes silence itself. This is an encounter with the human condition poles apart from the intellectualism of Maimonides.

The simple (or not so simple) acceptance of the way things are for human beings resonates in the final chapter of Ecclesiastes (12:1–8):

> So appreciate your vigor in the days of your youth,
>> before those days of sorrow come and those years
>> arrive of which you will say, "I have no pleasure in
>> them"; before sun and light and moon and stars

grow dark, and clouds come back again after the
rain:
When the guards of the house become shaky,
And the men of valor are bent,
And the maids that grind, grown few, are idle,
And the ladies that peer through the windows grow dim;
And the doors to the street are shut—with the noise of
the hand mill growing fainter,
And the song of the bird growing feebler,
And the strains of music dying down;
When one is afraid of heights
And there is terror on the road—
For the almond tree may blossom,
The grasshopper be burdened,
And the caper bush may bud again;
But man sets out for his eternal abode,
With the mourners all around in the street.
Before the silver cord snaps
And the golden bowl crashes
The jar is shattered at the spring,
And the jug is smashed at the cistern.
And the dust returns to the ground as it was,
And the life breath returns to God Who bestowed it.
Utter futility—said Kohelet—all is futile!

Ecclesiastes (Kohelet in Hebrew), the figure after whom
the book is named, mourns the loss of vitality and inexorable
decline that comes with age. Melancholy compounds vulnerability. His final wisdom is austere and tragic; all is transient

and futile (hevel), like the "life breath" (ruaḥ) that returns to
God. There is no apprehension of a world to come, no fear or
promise of eternity.

The stark disenchantment of this vision was too much for
the biblical editors to bear. Already in antiquity an epilogue
was added, counseling caution in treating the "sayings of the
wise," and urging that what really matters "when all is said and
done is to revere God and observe His commandments. For
this applies to all mankind: that God will call every creature to
account for everything unknown, be it good or bad" (Ecc.
12:13).

The pious message does not so much refute the book's deflationary perspective as decline to endorse it fully.[83] That is
fitting. As sober as Kohelet's wisdom might be for individuals
in their solitariness, it can hardly inspire a community to per-
severe. Neither escape into contemplation nor tragic resignation fully suits the Jewish image of the person.

Defending Personhood

This sketch of a Jewish manifest image of the person has em-
phasized the moral dimensions of human nature. To a certain
extent, then, it avoids reckoning with aspects of contemporary inquiries into human nature. One central aspect is the
"hard problem" of consciousness: the ability of conscious beings to experience awareness of their own bodily and psychic
processes. Why did natural selection favor a being capable of
internal self-awareness? Would it not have sufficed to perceive
the world, register sensations, and react in an appropriate

manner? What advantage accrues from being able to experience oneself experiencing one's sensations? Why did consciousness evolve?

Evolutionary psychologists and philosophers who pursue these questions often find it useful to imagine an alternative to a being with consciousness: a "zombie." Consider a GPS device in a car. It "perceives" the location of the car in terms of a set of coordinates, the vector of the car, its speed, and so forth. It then makes "decisions" about how the driver should proceed to some preestablished destination. Now imagine a vastly ramped-up device that functions like a human being across a wide range of cognitive tasks. The device doesn't just navigate; it reads books, has conversations, moves about robotically, and exercises skills like flytying or omelet making. In short, while being no more conscious than a GPS, it can do pretty much what human beings do.

Anyone who has seen a dystopic science-fiction movie will have no problem imagining such a zombie.[84] Although it functions like a human being, it is not a human being—not only because it is made of silicon chips, aluminum, and plastic, but because it lacks consciousness. You can have a (limited) conversation with an automated telephone system, but it has no experience of *what it is like* to be what it is—precisely the experience, on Nagel's telling, that can be said to distinguish the conscious from the nonconscious being.[85] Presumably, evolution selected genes that built a brain architecture supporting consciousness, but exactly why is unclear. No less apparent, from the perspective of cognitive science, is whether that consciousness is central or epiphenomenal. In other words, is consciousness what must be explained or just a kind of residue? Proponents of the latter view believe that once you've explained every relevant mental function in neurobiological terms, there is nothing left to clarify; the experience of what it is like to be something melts into air.

These issues do not concern the Jewish sources, which work at another level. They presume that we are conscious beings. They take the existence of the subject, the human person, put it at the heart of human nature, and treat it as bedrock reality. As well they should, I think. Whatever is going on in the subbasement of our biology, the first-person subject, as we have seen, is basic and can't be coherently eliminated. The scientistic story that seeks to dissolve the subject into the clatter of neural connections nonetheless offers reasons for why we should believe it. It asks us to be complicit in our own conceptual disassembly—an odd, even paradoxical move. The Jewish sources are far from this world picture. They are concerned not with what consciousness *is* but instead with how we *use* our consciousness as responsible beings. To say that we are made in the image of God is not meant to explain how conscious mind evolved, nor should it impede research into such scientific or philosophical questions. What it should do is to orient our moral practice by sharpening our reasons for treating one another and ourselves with dignity.

Some contemporary debunkers, of a scientistic cast of mind, claim that with the demise of traditional conceptions of personhood or selfhood, the need for a new ethics arises. They would substitute an allegedly scientific ethics for our current amalgam of traditions, religious and secular. The motivating idea is that once the Jewish and Christian views of human nature, especially of its dignity and sacred worth, collapse, the role and meaning of personhood must change, with the requisite alterations in moral theory and practice. Our elevation of ourselves into the most valuable species, for example, is groundless. Animals, at least higher ones, who suffer pain and have recognizably conscious minds should have rights equal to ours. Indeed, severely damaged infants might have less value and hence fewer rights than fully functioning animals. Contemporary thinkers such as Peter Singer therefore urge us to substitute a new, scientifically informed morality for a traditional one—the latter having lost, they assume, its authority to pronounce persuasively on human experience. But such thinkers underestimate the difficulty of vaulting from scientific *explanations* of being human, with their vaunted value neutrality, to moral *prescriptions* for human beings. That too is an overreach of scientism. It is one thing to describe and explain the world, as science does. It is another to draw normative conclusions from those factual descriptions. Even when it comes to digging down into the deepest layers of our biological being, it is one thing to explain the normative—as evolutionary psychology tries to do—and quite another to offer a normative explanation.

We might be told, for instance, that a highly social primate species, such as our own, evolved to practice kin altruism. Suppressing our own needs for those of selective others helped us to survive. As such, the genes of those hominids who excelled in altruistic behavior were passed on while those of more selfish, less social hominids died out. But how does one get from that descriptive/explanatory story to an account of why we should keep our promises or why we should share with others? That certain practices helped remote ancestors to survive does not rise to a moral justification for why they should be continued or why they should prevail when a conflict of values obtains. Science picks out causes. Ethics works in the space of reasons. Using reason to explore, persuade, argue, convince, and defend is worlds away from the causal systems that science illumines. We can't quite get from one to the other, notwithstanding scientism's robust faith assertions. For that, you need persons—moral subjects who can't be eliminated.

Jewish approaches to human nature or, as Heschel would have it, being human are compatible with scientific ones. It's the scientistic interpretations that give offense. The biblical emphasis on the unity of the person as a somatic-psychic whole, which the rabbis both sustain and challenge, resonates with contemporary neuroscience. Antonio Damasio, for one, views the development of human consciousness as the expansion of the capacity to feel. Feelings such as pleasure and pain are a kind of perception of the internal and external state of our own bodies. The brain both maps these feeling-producing states and constructs metarepresentations of its own perceptual process.[86] Thought, in other words, is thoroughly grounded in corporeality—in perception, sensation, and the mapping of body states. Damasio uses Spinoza's idea of the mind as the "idea of the human body."[87] The scientific turn away from the dichotomy between mind and body provides an occasion for Jewish thought to reappropriate and reformulate its patrimony—a unitive account of human nature in which body, feeling, and thinking rise and fall together.

Two other issues emanating from neuroscience seem less compatible with Jewish perspectives. One, the problem of free will, will occupy us in the next chapter. Here I can conclude with the second: the place or nonplace of selfhood. As we have seen, a concept of the self as a responsible being is critical to Jewish thought about being human. Contemporary neuroscience, however, discredits the concept of selfhood to the degree that the word self implies something stable, a kind of entity.

A neuroscientist or neurophilosopher might say that the modern concept of a self descends from an earlier religious or folk notion of the soul. Both self and soul were held to be composed of occult mental stuff, different in kind from the extended physical stuff that made up the external world. Mental stuff, memorably derided by the British philosopher Gilbert Ryle as the ghost in the machine, has no place in the physicalist universe of brain science. Self, self-consciousness, qualitative states, and so on, must be reduced from the language of subjective experience to that of neuronal activity.

The neuroscientific claim is that self designates such capacities of the brain as the ability to map the internal homeostatic states of the body, the position of the body at rest and in motion in space, its responses to internal and external stimuli, the ability to initiate muscular exertion, notice feelings, become aware on a metalevel of neuronal activity taking place at a more primary level, and so forth. Self thus captures a plethora of brain activity occurring in parallel-processed information states; there is no unified, executive center, no internal "Cartesian theater," as Daniel Dennett calls it.[88] Consciousness per se is not a unified process but instead a "multitude of widely distributed specialized systems and disunited processes."[89] Self is a catchall for a teeming throng of mental processes; it is not a tag for a single thing.

Nonetheless, we feel that we have—that we *are*—a unified center of thought, decision, memory, and executive function. A neuroscientist might say this is because one of those specialized systems, the left-hemisphere interpreter (as the cognitive neuroscientist Michael Gazzaniga calls it), has been selected by evolution to produce such a representation. The left-hemisphere interpreter infers causal connections among events, thereby generating explanations. When we perceive a fresh scar on someone's face, for example, we immediately jump to speculate about how it got there. Or at least our left-brain interpreter does. In this reading, selfhood is a kind of narrative explanation arising from an information-shaping activity that brings coherence to the parallel, diverse, ramified activities of the brain. Gazzaniga puts it this way: "Our subjective awareness arises out of our dominant left hemisphere's unrelenting quest to explain these bits and pieces that have popped into consciousness."[90] Presumably, those prehistoric hominids who, as a result of random genetic mutations, acquired the illusion of having an executive control center in their heads fared better than their competitors and reproduced more effectively. This makes every human being who fancies that he or she has a self into a descendant of those lucky hominids.

Is selfhood, then, like Otto von Bismarck's quip about politics and sausages—that is, you shouldn't look too closely at how they are made? One could argue that a neuroscientific account of the neural nature of selfhood does not necessarily undermine our *experience* of selfhood. Analogously, a neurobiological account of vision doesn't alter how we see things. But there is a level at which such an account becomes problematic, and that is when it dismisses experience altogether. This occurs through the global equation of mind with brain, reduction of mental states to neuronal synaptic activity, and elimination of the bedrock existence of thoughts, beliefs, desires, and intentions in favor of firings, processing, computation, and function.[91]

To the extent that neuroscience is set on a relentless march against the integrity of the first-person perspective, Jewish and other understandings of being human are duty bound to resist. This march was not initiated by neuroscience. Reductionism is deep in the culture of science. All the arrows of causality, the physicist Steven Weinberg claims, point downward to physics, the level at which things are ultimately explained and at which manifest images are shown to be appearances rather than realities.

Jewish thought, by contrast, appeals to our conception of ourselves as persons. It takes that conception to be reliable and necessary. It is compatible with the view that selfhood is an emergent property of neurobiological processes. The fact that we are composed of tens of trillions of cells, each one a living creature of a kind, does not do away with *us*. We are not mere sums of those trillions, but rather unique occasions of their interaction. Were it not for the reality of the whole, continually maintaining and directing the parts, the parts themselves would not exist. Indeed, the very concept of a part is misleading here; the whole is a dynamic, organized process, not an assemblage of discrete parts.[92] Consciousness has its own arrows of causation.

A specifically Jewish view would also move beyond the *phenomenon* of selfhood into its *significance*, into the meaning of personhood. It would claim that being human (that is, a person who is responsible for his or her portion of the world) is to represent God in the world, to cocreate with God. It is to find existence good—a gift to which one should respond in gratitude. In a famous poem, Philip Larkin declares, "Man hands on misery to man. It deepens as a coastal shelf. Get out as early as you can and don't have any kids yourself."[93] Judaism differs. Misery is real enough, but so is goodness and blessing. We hand these on to our children, and if we are worthy, we thereby deepen them.

The elderly patriarch Jacob was bitter in his last days. "Few and hard have been the years of my life, nor do they come up to the life spans of my fathers during their sojourns" (Gen. 47:9). Nonetheless, Jacob's final act is not to curse God and die but instead to exhibit intense and specific concern for the future of his children as well as the people they will form. The Jewish stance is always to affirm the blessing of new life and possibility despite the fact that the world goes according to its accustomed way.

Are Persons Free to Choose?

Painted in capital letters on the side of a building at Broadway and Seventy-Second Street in New York City is a message: "Depression is a Flaw in Chemistry, not Character." Accompanying it is a phone number to call for further information. These words convey an element of truth, but they raise more questions than they aim to resolve.

The message tells you that it's not your fault that you are depressed; instead, the fault lies in some chemical imbalance in your brain, upstream in your genes, or in the interaction of your brain and genes with your environment. Its words are thus meant to comfort, relieve self-blame, foster self-acceptance, and invite depressed individuals to consider medical treatment that will fight chemistry with, presumably, better chemistry.

Although depression (melancholia) has a long history, going back to Hippocrates, as a medical phenomenon, it straddled the medical and the moral realms. Today's approach, though, embeds it in the medical frame of reference without remainder. This move is already implicit in the use of the clinical term depression—as opposed to melancholy or sadness. In Judaism, the Talmud teaches that God's presence (sh'khina) does not rest on one who is gloomy (B. Pesaḥim 117a). For early Christianity, sadness (*tristitia*) was either a sin or a condition that gives rise to sin, especially the sin of *acedia*: sloth, indifference, and despair. One was called to assume responsibility for one's sinful condition and turn the passivity of sadness into the activity of love. A whole field of battle opens up—a field on which the individual struggles with vice and aims for virtue.

With medicalization, all this largely disappears. Depression as a "flaw in chemistry" does not eliminate the concept of responsibility entirely, but instead shifts its focus elsewhere. Suffering from depression is not blameworthy; failing to seek treatment may be. An alcoholic or drug addict is no longer accused of the vice of gluttony—addiction is a chemical flaw, not a character flaw—yet one is still expected to do something about it. If the goal used to be a deep personal transformation in terms of a religious or moral ideal, the aim nowadays is normalcy, proper functioning, and self-acceptance. In both cases, an idea of human nature operates; both instances acknowledge the profound role played by internal constraints on human freedom.

Rich literatures in antiquity and the Middle Ages ponder how a truly human life might be achieved in the face of such natural limitations. Judaism in particular is no stranger to the theme of how the natural challenges the ideal. Can these religious sources continue to address the issues as they are framed in our time?

The basic problem remains one of free will versus determinism, but the accent is different. Some Jewish sources are well aware of the problematic status of human freedom in the world—problematic not because of the (as many contemporary philosophers see it) closed causal order of nature but rather because of God's sovereignty. Can God be said to have pulled away from controlling the world and cleared a space in which human beings are genuinely free to choose? If so, God's omnipotence is diminished and impugned. The same goes for God's omniscience: if humans are free to decide for themselves what they will do, how can God know what they will do until they do it? And if God already knows what they will do, where is their freedom of decision?

Conundrums like these preoccupied our medieval ancestors; I will consider several examples later in this chapter.[1] But first we need to get a sense of the problem as it is spoken of today.

Persons and Causes

Let us return again to the quote from Crick: "You, your joys and your sorrows, your memories and your ambitions, your sense of personal identity and free will, are in fact no more than the behavior of a vast assembly of nerve cells and their associated molecules."[2]

Wilson, Crick's eminent fellow biologist, frames the same thought in somewhat more delicate terms:

> The great paradox of determinism and free will, which has held the attention of the wisest of philosophers and

psychologists for generations, can be phrased in biological terms as follows: if our genes are inherited and our environment is a train of physical events set in motion before we were born, how can there be a truly independent agent within the brain? The agent itself is created by the interaction of the genes and the environment. It would appear that our freedom is only a self-delusion.[3]

What these scientists are saying is that consciousness and judgment are products of the activity of the brain, and the brain is a physical object that perforce obeys the laws of physics and biochemistry. The genes that code for the proteins forming brain tissue have a history; they are the products of long causal chains marked by survival and adaptation. Although we may not yet understand how all this works, we recognize *in principle* what an explanation would look like. How, then, could something as unnatural as freedom—a seeming zone of radical indeterminacy, aloof from determining causal chains—exist?

Given the materialist picture of the world favored by scientism, it seems impossible. But if that materialist, causal-closure picture predominates, what then happens to our stubborn belief in the status of humans as conscious beings and moral agents who exercise responsibility in the world as well as can be held accountable for their choices? What then happens to personhood?

Some thinkers hope to have discovered a solution to this puzzle in the findings of quantum physics. Here after all is a domain, within nature itself, where the concept of causality seems to break down. Could uncaused events at the quantum microlevel be seen to resonate in free will events at the level of human consciousness? Although determinism looked like a formidable problem when classical physics was the best available description of the world, quantum mechanics introduces the possibility of radical indeterminacy and therefore perhaps a source for a strong account of free will. Still, as Philip Kitcher and others have pointed out, it is not at all clear how this could work. Kitcher writes:

> Imagine a random robot—call it Oscar—whose limbs move in accordance with a sequence of random events. Inside Oscar's head is a collection of pigeonholes; each pigeonhole contains a radioactive nucleus; the nucleus sits on a platform, attached to Oscar's limbs with sensitive springs and levers; as the nucleus decays, the platform moves and one of Oscar's limbs jerks. The sequence of Oscar's action is not determined. Yet Oscar is not free.[4]

Indeterminacy would result in randomness, which is the antithesis of free action.[5] Freedom of the will has to do not with random, unpredictable actions (if the "action" could even be said to apply) but instead with the intentional direction of action to accord with beliefs, desires, rational considerations, and so on. The person must not be taken out of the process.

Whatever the relevance of quantum mechanics might turn out to be, something else seems wrong with this general picture—and that something is its basic characterization of free will. Do we really need to think of it as a zone of radical indeterminacy? Is it not rather a special kind of *causality*? That at least has been the hypothesis of some important modern thinkers, among them Hume. Hume's view, which amounts to a kind of determinism, is directed against the iconic perspective of Descartes, who represented a full-blown indeterminism.

For Descartes, the will is a feature of the soul, which is "by its nature so free that it can't ever be constrained."[6] The soul exists within its own sphere as an extensionless, thinking substance; one of its self-generated activities is volition, which aims either at a physical goal like walking or a mental goal such as (in Descartes's example) loving God. With respect to its own realm, moreover, the will is unconstrained—like a wholly free, sovereign, creative deity.

There is something wrong with Descartes's picture— namely, its basic assumption that there exists a force, the will, which answers to none of the laws of nature. Placing the will beyond nature, his rhetoric notwithstanding, Descartes puts human volition beyond the possibility of scientific investigation. Descartes's view rests on a thoroughgoing dualism of the very kind that modern science rejects. Repudiating that dualism a century after Descartes, Hume proposed a more empirical approach. For Hume, the will is not separate, sovereign, and free but itself subject to causation instead. What Hume sought to ascertain was the *kind* of causation that is at work when we make the choices we do.[7]

According to Hume, what we really mean when we say we have free choice is that we have acted not by accident but rather deliberately, that the action is our own, and that we experienced no compulsion or coercion—in other words, that we acted on the basis of decisions for which we can be held accountable. Such decisions are made by us, but within a subtle network of causes, not within a cause-free zone. Desires, beliefs, and other motivations play a causal role; they determine choices. To Hume, the kind of freedom envisioned by Descartes is a chimera; the only freedom available is one compatible with causality. Hume's view belongs to a cluster of positions called compatibilism.

One influential contemporary version of compatibilism, that of Harry Frankfurt, stresses our decision to accept or, more precisely, endorse a choice as our own regardless of how it has arisen. Other animals have desires—higher animals may even deliberate about them—but only human beings can incorporate (or repudiate) their desires into a conception of themselves. Frankfurt argues that we manifest free will when we identify ourselves with our first-order desires. Our desires come from we know not where; processes unknown to us engender them. But if we can endorse our desires—if we can *desire* to desire something or other—then we have manifested the only kind of free will there is.[8] Hence, if I desire to go to a movie, and on reflection, accept that desire as legitimate, valuable, and worthwhile, then I have made that desire mine, and I go to the movie voluntarily and freely. I accept or endorse a conception of myself as someone who finds aesthetic enjoyment in moviegoing. If, by contrast, I desire to smoke crack cocaine, but also know that it is injurious (and so have another first-order desire not to smoke), whether I have freedom of the will depends on whether I can identify fully with one of these conflicting desires and incorporate it successfully into my conception of the person I want to be. Do I desire to be the kind of person who is a crack smoker or abstainer? Insofar as this is a problem for me, with which I have to struggle, I find my free will in the struggle to form my self-conception.

For a compatibilist of this stripe, freedom does not mean acting in the absence of strong causative desires or constraints but rather in their presence, and building one's sense of oneself in the face of them. Freedom is a kind of intentional endorsement that brings wholeness, that preserves the whole person as a moral agent. A Cartesian-style indeterminist might regard this as sham freedom; the compatibilist considers it as adequate to what we mean when we say that someone has acted of their own free will.

Compatibilism relies on rather flexible ideas of freedom and agency. These become problematic, however, when the discussion is framed in the terms of neuroscience, which relegates the causal background, the realm where our supposedly free choices are made, to the level of neurobiology—the same level at which our first-order desires originate. Given this, we may feel as a matter of personal experience that we have made our choices at some remove from a causally determined framework, but for neuroscientists that is never the case. It is an illusion, if a powerful and useful one in the sense of being evolved or adaptive.

The difficulty of sustaining compatibilism in a neuroscientific mode is manifest in the experiments of Benjamin Libet, who tried to show that "decisions" are made at a neuronal level before the conscious mind becomes aware of them. His contention is that as opposed to formulating desires and *then* enacting them, we become conscious, fractions of a second *after* it has been initiated, of an incipient action. "The brain has acted before its person is conscious of it."[9] In that case, we do not have freedom of will in the sense of being able to initiate our desires. But we do have, as Gazzaniga calls it, "freedom of won't." That is, we can still select and control our actions "either by permitting the movement that arises out of an unconsciously initiated process or by 'vetoing the progression to actual motor activation.'"[10]

Yet does this not vitiate Hume's criterion of free will—namely, that I accept my action as my own, not as an act that I have been compelled to perform? And what about Frankfurt's criterion—that I at least identify myself, on reflection, with a first-order desire? With the very concepts of selfhood and agency being pulled out from under us by neuroscience, the answers are unclear. How are we to recognize ourselves as human persons once free will has been translated into a filtering mechanism functioning ex post facto to modulate preconscious brain activity? How can we continue to recognize ourselves as persons versus complex neurobiological processes?

Such views are troubling even to the neuroscientists and philosophers who propound them. At the end of the day, they still have to go home, and live with themselves and others. That is, they can't discount the reality of personhood in their own lives. The philosopher John Searle maintains that the first-person experience of free will can't be eliminated. Even those who think it is an illusion cannot act on that presupposition. In Searle's example, the strict neurodeterminist cannot go into a restaurant and, instead of making a choice from the menu, say to the waiter, "Look, I am a determinist; I'll just wait and see what I order."[11] This would be self-impugning and a performative contradiction. The refusal to exercise free will would only be intelligible to you *as a choice*, as an *exercise* of free will. Free will, like the personhood with which it is associated, is therefore necessary to our self-conception. We cannot succeed in conceiving of ourselves as persons without it.

Some have tried to weaken the hold of the free will/personhood picture of human experience by recourse to evolutionary biology. The reasoning goes like this. Just as chimps and other social animals rely on punishment, exclusion, and shunning behavior to enforce norms that are necessary for group survival, human beings, too, are naturally selected/genetically programmed to maintain such practices. As a rule, free will in the case of other primates does not trouble us; on the contrary, we accept that their policing practices are entirely natural and confer a survival advantage. So why not do the same with humans? In Patricia Churchland's view, we should simply "naturalize" the social policing of human action. Ascribing praise and blame, fixing responsibility—this is just what our kind of highly social, highly developed primate does. There is nothing mysterious about it.[12]

Whatever truth there may be in the story that Churchland tells, her view preserves the practices that constitute moral life at the cost of gutting them of their meaning. She can preserve group norms along with assignments of praise and blame, but she cannot preserve the persons who enact or deserve them.

An impersonal perspective overwhelms the personal one. The causal story behind a practice, such as punishing or shunning, doesn't reach to the *internal reasons* that real persons would give to justify or interpret it.[13] Whatever the story that evolutionary biology tells about why we do what we do, we are still left to make sense of what we do within our own, moral form of life. Biological causes do not count as moral reasons. When we engage in moral life—such as when, for example, we judge the actions of another—we are not simply playing out a genetically determined script, a page taken from the life of the higher primates. We are experiencing the meaning and significance of our practices and norms as we enact them. One cannot say that the supposed evolutionary cause of our practices trump the reasons by which we explain and justify them to ourselves as well as others. One cannot coherently substitute a third-person account of moral life from the first-person experience of it without imploding moral life per se.

Gazzaniga, a scientist who tries to maintain the salience of recognizable human agency in a neuroscientific context, takes a different tack. For him, the *individual* brain is the wrong place to look. Agency and responsibility are *social* categories. "The way to think about responsibility is that it is an interaction between people, a social contract." Similarly with consciousness and thought, which are "emergent properties found in the group interactions of many brains." Responsibility and freedom, according to Gazzaniga, are not located within the brain; they emerge in the space "between brains."[14] But for the anatomical language, Buber would agree. The self, for Buber, comes into being in encounter and relationship with others.

Personhood arises in the realm of what Buber calls "the interhuman."[15]

Gazzaniga's tack is promising, though perhaps it too over-reaches. Holding agents responsible is, of course, a social prac-tice—a public feature of a shared form of life. Yet Gazzaniga is saying more. He is not just locating where freedom, person-hood, moral agency, and responsibility take place; he is giving a reductive account of their origins, claiming that the interac-tion of multiple brains produces behaviors with significant adaptive consequences. We are still being asked to find our-selves in our brains. What pertains to personhood is no longer reduced to just one brain but rather to the interaction of many brains. Brains still seem to occupy the place where persons used to be.

Is this view intelligible from a personal vantage point? Per-haps our moral practices and sense of moral personhood are not weakened by such an account any more than our convic-tion of the solidity of tables is weakened by an atomic account of matter in terms of which tables are mostly empty space. Per-haps. But how, in the end, can we find ourselves in a story that is about our brains rather than ourselves?

In what follows, I will trace some steps that Jewish thinkers have taken in grappling with questions of free will and deter-minism, with the aim of sketching a Jewish conception both committed to personhood and open to science. Although ancient and medieval Jewish texts are obviously innocent of the problems of neuroscience, they are fully aware of a range of considerations that tend toward a deterministic metaphys-ics. Astrology, for instance, with its notion of stellar and planetary influence on physical traits as well as attitudes, behavior, and destiny, was widespread among medieval Jews, despite Maimonides's forceful denunciation of it.[16] So too were a Hellenistic conception of medicine based on the balance of humors in the body as well as the thesis that personality types, moods, psychological tendencies, and so forth are governed by physical substances.[17] Neither of these analytic frameworks counts as science today, but both of them provide occasions for thinking directly about whether or to what degree the will is free. And that, as we have seen, is crucial to our sense of ourselves as persons.

Free Will, Determinism, and Judaism

The Bible seems to assume a robust picture of human agency. Verses like "shun evil and do good, seek amity and pursue it" (Ps. 34:13) and "I have put before you life and death, blessing and curse. Choose life, if you and your offspring would live" (Deut. 30:19) presuppose the ability to discriminate among alternative possibilities along with the capacity to choose the best one. The picture is not darkened by worries about whether choice is truly free, persons are the real agents of their choice, or it is right to hold them responsible for their decisions. The Bible seems (naively?) to presuppose all that.

Still, if we look around a bit, we find instances where this straightforward and sanguine view is qualified. In Exodus 20:5, after the proscription of making idols and bowing down to serve them, God says, "For I the Lord your God am an impassioned God, visiting the guilt of the parents upon the children, upon the third and upon the fourth generations of those who reject Me, but showing kindness to the thousandth generation of those who love Me and keep My commandments." The text places individuals within their family lineages, and envisions their reward or punishment as dependent on their ancestors' behavior. Apparently, an individual's fate can be determined on collective and vicarious versus strictly personal grounds. Or can it? The phrases "those who reject Me" and "those who love Me" would seem to suggest that the reward and punishment of descendants is contingent on whether *they* act in conformity with the actions of their ancestors—and this is exactly how later Jewish tradition reads the verse. That is, the text qualifies itself by introducing an element of individual responsibility.

Nonetheless, the dimension—or fear—of collective reward or punishment remains salient in later Israelite experience. In Jeremiah 31:29, for example, the Judeans who will suffer the collapse of their state at the hands of the invading Babylonians blame their ancestors for their misfortune. The immoral acts of the forebearers will be requited on their hapless descendants. This is captured in a proverb that was widespread among the people of that generation: "Parents have eaten sour grapes and children's teeth are blunted."

Jeremiah 31:30, however, offers a sharp moral critique of this view: "Everyone shall die for his own sins; whoever eats sour grapes, his teeth shall be blunted." So, too, Ezekiel 18:3–4 in the next generation: "As I live—declares the Lord God—this proverb shall no longer be current among you in Israel. Consider, all lives are Mine; the life of the parent and the life of the child are both Mine. The person who sins, only he shall die." Both Jeremiah and Ezekiel emphasize the "robust" picture of individual agency and responsibility by de-emphasizing an earlier vision of collective, intergenerational responsibility. And in fact the Torah also comes to reject that collective vision, as in Deuteronomy 24:16: "Parents shall not be put to death for children, nor children be put to death for parents: a person [*ish*] shall be put to death only for his own crime."

Throughout the biblical stories, the tension persists between the individuated and collective view of moral agency— or as we might put it, between the voluntarist and determinist perspective. Although the biblical authors move toward the liberty of moral agents to choose, a sense remains that human choice is also determined by other forces, preeminently God's foreknowledge and foreordaining of human history. In the Joseph story, say, after Joseph reveals himself to his astonished brothers, he tells them "not to be distressed" or reproach themselves for having sold him into slavery, since "it was to save life that God sent me ahead of you. . . . God has sent me ahead of you to ensure your survival on earth. . . . So, it was not you who sent me here, but God" (Gen. 45:5–8). (Curiously, the brothers don't quite buy it [Gen. 50:15–18]. Their lingering sense of guilt attests to their belief in their own agency.)

Operating here is what the biblical scholar Yehezkel Kaufman calls a dual causality.[18] Human beings think that their plans and choices are their own, but God is working behind the scenes, shaping both daily life and the broad sweep of history in some mysterious manner to affect His own desired outcomes. This pattern is pervasive not only in early biblical books where the miraculous is patent but also in later books like Esther, where the presence of God is entirely indirect and recondite.[19]

How much human agency is possible in a universe governed by a divine sovereign? To what extent are we humans divinely programmed robots? This question is evoked by the story of the exodus when the pharaoh repeatedly refuses to let the Israelites go. He refuses because, as God tells Moses, "I will harden Pharaoh's heart, that I may multiply My signs and marvels in the land of Egypt" (Exod. 7:3). Even if the pharaoh wants to let the Israelites go, God will stiffen his resolve to keep them enslaved.

This raises an obvious moral problem. Is it unjust of God to punish the pharaoh for his actions insofar as he is denied free choice? Although this problem exercised later Jewish exegetes, it seems not to have greatly troubled the biblical author. Then again, the structure of the narrative may suggest a subtle authorial recognition of the problem. God's hardening of the pharaoh's heart does not begin until the sixth plague. "For the first five plagues," Nahum Sarna observes, "the pharaoh's obduracy is a product *of his own volition*," and only afterward does his agency decline as God eliminates his ability to choose. In this sense, the pharaoh has already chosen his own fate.[20]

The Bible often presents persons as buffeted by forces— such as the sin-inducing demon crouching at the door in the Cain story (Gen. 4:7)—they must control. These forces do not eliminate free will, but it is challenged. In the Book of Judges, the Israelites are caught in a pattern of sin, punishment, redemption, and relapse: they collectively struggle to live according to the covenant with God, collectively fail to do so, and become collectively oppressed by the native peoples. A charismatic leader then saves them. But this divinely initiated and humanly effectuated deliverance is only temporary.

The cyclic pattern found in Judges gives expression to the sense that human beings are not ultimately in control of their destiny. The Israelite vision is not *wholly* fatalistic: God, after all, controls history, and God may be moved by repentance and righteousness. Nevertheless, there is an awareness of being caught up in the play of larger forces that we can scarcely understand, let alone control. This recognition is familiar to moderns as well. Even in a secular age, we understand ourselves to be located within humanly contrived institutions and humanly generated forces, such as the economy or state, over which we have limited control, if any. We become creatures of our creations.

Neither the Bible nor the rabbis theorize the exact balance between human agency and the divinely originated determination of events. For that, we must await the medieval philosophers. A famous passage in the Mishnah, "All is foreseen but freedom of choice [*reshut*] is given" (Avot 3:19), propounds though does not resolve the paradox. Similarly, the Talmud maintains that "all is in the hands of heaven except for the fear of heaven" (B. Berakhot 33b).[21] Following Talmudic precedents, Rashi clarifies what this implies: all that happens to a person comes from God. Whether one is tall or short, poor or rich, wise or foolish, white or black—all is in the hands of heaven. Yet whether one is righteous or wicked—

that is not determined by heaven but instead is in one's own hand.[22]

Rashi's line of reasoning is somewhat like Frankfurt's concept of second-order volition: the desire to desire. Our principal characteristics are to some significant extent determined, but our most consequential moral choices are subject to our control. We can choose to approve or disapprove of the desires we have or persons we are.

Reason, guided by divine grace, can return us to the proper way. In the face of the contingency of our situation and accidental nature of some aspects of our personhood, we need to form the right desires and incorporate them as motives into our self-conception. Ideally, we come to recognize what good motives are through intellectual discernment. Jews, after all, pray three times daily for "knowledge, understanding, and insight" so that they can return to God's Torah. In the formula where this request is articulated, we see the unresolved ambiguity of the rabbinic stance. The prayer is for intellectual gifts that allow a searching mind to seek and find the right path, but the very setting—a prayer—acknowledges the inadequacy of unassisted human effort. Attaining the fear of heaven needs the help of heaven.

Sometimes it needs the aid of earthly beings as well. An important instance is found in the Talmud (B. Arakhin 21a). The Mishnah rules that a court may coerce a recalcitrant husband who refuses to give his wife a legal document of divorce (*get*) to do so until he acts "voluntarily"; he is compelled to act freely, as it were. Typically, one would find a contradiction here: coerced agreement is no agreement at all. But the rabbis do not view it that way. The court is helping the husband to come to the right decision, even if he opposes it and experiences the court's assistance as coercion. The right decision is in accord with what a later age might call the husband's best self—the self that would want to do "what is right and good in the sight of the Lord" (Deut. 6:18).

The idea that freedom consists of thinking and acting in accordance with a higher power is a familiar one in Jewish sources. For the medieval philosophers (as later for Spinoza, Judaism's great modern heretic), that higher power is the God-given capacity of reason. The medieval philosophers make allowance for a wide variety of determining causal factors, reaching deep down into human nature. Nonetheless, reason can correct for these factors and guide the individual person toward perfection through the discipline of self-command.

Three medieval thinkers who take this course are Solomon ibn Gabirol (d. 1058), Bahya ibn Pakuda (d. 1156), and Maimonides. These three, as I will present them, are compatibilists. A fourth, Crescas, moves beyond compatibilism to a more robust determinism. Despite the conventional view that Judaism enjoins a strong commitment to free will, the four medieval thinkers show the degree to which traditional Judaism can be reconciled with a compatibilist or even stricter position. The point is not to dissolve our personal experience of free will—that remains crucial. It rather is to show that the experience of persons who take themselves to be free and responsible beings remains intact whatever the underlying physics and metaphysics turns out to be.

Ibn Gabirol accepts the view, inherited from Galen, that the physical elements (air, water, earth, and fire) in their combinations determine the humors (blood, white gall, black gall, and yellow gall) of which the body is composed. The combinations create conditions of warmth and cold, moistness and dryness, and those conditions determine the abilities and operations of the five senses. Ibn Gabirol's original contribution is to assert that each sense determines four of a person's character traits, with these four being made up of two pairs of opposites (or sometimes, four loosely related traits). Thus, sight originates and sustains pride and meekness, modesty and impudence. Hearing gives rise to love and hate, mercy and cruelty. Smell entails anger, goodwill, jealousy, and alertness. And so forth. The rational soul, which is a pure creation of God and incapable of evil, can discipline, train, and order the five physical senses and the character traits dependent on them, thereby enabling us to bring our humor- and sense-based character under conscious control. The majority of ibn Gabirol's treatise is a manual for the control of each of the twenty traits.[23]

It is important to ibn Gabirol's linkage of character traits with particular senses that the senses be understood as *generating* the traits. This is a somewhat perplexing claim, but a clue to his thinking may be found in his treatment of taste. Although, he writes, the sense of taste may be ranked lower than the other four senses, it is actually the most important of all.[24] One can live without sight as a blind person or without hearing as a deaf person, but one cannot live without taste. Why not? Because, for ibn Gabirol, taste generates appetite, and we cannot live without eating—which is to say, without the underlying desire to eat.

Generalizing, we can see that ibn Gabirol construes the senses as sources of desire.[25] Hence, training the senses means curbing appetites, and inculcating proper dispositions and attitudes with respect to them. The character traits, in their vicious or virtuous dimensions, exist preformed *in potentia* in infants. They are made manifest *in actu* as a person ages. Already in youth, children incline toward one trait or another; by the age of twenty it is too late to do anything about them, and thus the significance of early training and education. In this program, like Aristotle before him and Maimonides after him, ibn Gabirol assigns a crucial role to habit. The senses along with their respective traits are expressive of the nutritive and appetitive (that is, the vegetative and animal) dimensions of the soul. These dimensions, which dominate the prerational life of youths, are highly deterministic. As people age, their rational souls assume greater power. But in most human beings the path has already been set; the moral traits have annealed into an inertia that can only be deflected with the greatest difficulty. Anticipating by centuries Kant's aphorism about the rough timber of humanity, Gabirol asserts, "A sprig may be made to stand erect before it is full grown but when it has become a tree, it is difficult to bend or move it."[26] Ibn Gabirol's work, then, is directed to the moral perfectionist who desires that reason should command habit, bearing in mind that reason affords no shortcuts, and that no deus ex machina can be relied on to intervene and do the work of moral transformation for us.

Although his naturalist theory may not be persuasive to us today, ibn Gabirol sensitively balances determinism and freedom. On the determinist side, the senses and their associated character traits reflect the operations of the underlying vegetative and animal dimensions of the soul. These are prerational. The traits are both inborn and strengthened (or weakened) by upbringing and habit. Natural conditions determine what the traits are; biographical and historical contingencies determine how they develop as well as prevail. Much of what human beings do seems to be hardwired. Yet on the voluntarist side, the rational soul, which is a gift of God and not subject to naturalistic conditioning factors, can orient the person away from vicious and base habits. Representing a zone of freedom in a deterministic universe, it can provide a rational override of impulse-driven traits through a gradual change in habit. There is something intuitively appealing about this picture. Even a thinker as dark as Sigmund Freud, who thought that human behavior was largely driven by repressed impulses generated by frustrated, intractable desires, held out the hope for enlightenment. Self-understanding, secured through analysis of one's psyche, might break the chains of invidious, involuntary neurotic habit.

Bahya, in his *Book of Direction to the Duties of the Heart*, treats the problem of free choice and determinism head-on in an extended philosophical dialogue between the mind and soul. The mind, replete with wisdom, fully grasps the divine design and purpose of the cosmos as well as the nature of reality. The soul represents the overall animate, intentional being that we recognize as a human person. The mind directs the soul, which in turn directs the body.[27]

In Baḥya's dialogue, the soul seeks guidance from the mind so that it can conduct itself appropriately. Among the matters that trouble the soul is the problem of freedom of choice and determinism. The soul's anxiety stems from its belief that the Bible affirms both divine governance of all things—"Whatever the Lord desires, He does in heaven and earth, in the seas and all the depths" (Ps. 135:6)—*and* freedom of choice.[28] Since these positions are mutually exclusive, what then should the soul believe?

The mind assures the soul that its dilemma is not only generated by biblical texts but also inherent in human experience as such. We sense the gap between our intentions and their effects. When things don't go as we intend, we intuit the presence of a higher power, God, who directs events and prevents us from realizing intentions that go against His will.[29] On the other hand, God allows us to inherit the consequences of our deeds.

The sages themselves (says the mind) are divided on this question. Some rabbis believe in voluntarism while others believe in determinism. The voluntarists (like Baḥya's predecessor, Saadya) have no problem affirming God's justice since, for them, reward and punishment both are fully contingent on free human choice. The determinists claim that God's justice is opaque to us. "God is just and does no evil. His promise of reward and punishment is true. It never fails. But our minds are too weak to grasp the meaning of His wisdom."[30]

Baḥya tries to find a third way. He aligns himself with another group of sages who hold to *both* views simultaneously. That is, one should act *as if* one had free will, while accepting all that happens, including one's own actions and their consequences, as God's will. He paraphrases the view of this third group as follows:

> The right way is to act in the belief that man's actions are entrusted to him, so that he earns reward or punishment, and to try to do everything that may benefit us before God both in this world and the next. On the other hand, we should rely on Him with the submission of those who know that all actions, movements, benefits, and misfortunes lie under God's rule and power and depend on His permission and decree, for He has the decisive argument against man, but man has no argument against his Creator.[31]

On the surface, this looks like no more than a counsel of prudence. Since either view could be the correct one, maintaining both would be cautious, if not terribly coherent. But Baḥya's approach goes beyond the prudential. He believes that both perspectives are not only necessary but mutually compatible too. They function at different levels, however. To put it into somewhat Kantian language, the voluntarist notion functions as a practical maxim—act as if your will determines your actions—while the determinist stance functions at a metaphysical level—God's power is sovereign over all events. This division of moral and metaphysical labor mitigates somewhat the conflict between the two views. Baḥya's metaphysical agnosticism further mitigates the conflict. What he really advocates is "setting aside the metaphysical question, as insoluble by human intelligence." In arguing that we should "presuppose free will in the moral/spiritual sphere and pre-destination in the realm of fortune and misfortune, he is offering, in the name of philosophy, not a decision between free-dom and fatalism but a criterion for determining the proper spheres of application for responsibility and resignation."[32] Baḥya, in other words, is like Kant in transposing the problem from a metaphysical to a moral register. If it is correct to call Baḥya a compatibilist, he is so in a practical sense: maintain-ing a belief in free choice is necessary for our moral and spiri-tual life, whatever the ultimate (unknowable) metaphysical disposition of the matter may be.

As Alexander Altmann puts it, Baḥya's formula "is more than a mere working hypothesis. It binds together his faith in divine justice with his religious experience of utter depen-dence on God."[33] Holding these two positions together is made possible (and necessary) by our ignorance of the ulti-mate state of things, and this ignorance is itself divinely willed. Indeed, it is ultimately to our benefit, since "our minds are weak and our discrimination short.... Were it to our advan-tage to know this secret, the Creator would have revealed it to us."[34] Baḥya is willing to live with the mystery. God's ways are recondite, but personhood is preserved.

Maimonides treats the problem in several different ways. In his legal code, the *Mishneh Torah*, he endorses a robust volun-tarism. He modifies that view somewhat in *Eight Chapters*, a

131

freestanding introduction to his commentary on Mishnah
Avot (The ethics of the fathers). He then complicates the picture a bit in his masterwork, *The Guide of the Perplexed*, where
he seems to insinuate a determinist view. Given the vexed
question of whether or to what extent Maimonides is an eso-
teric thinker, who veils his true views from the masses, is the
last of these perspectives his true belief, and are the voluntarist
positions the ones he thinks the masses need to sustain their
piety?

Since there is no simple way to resolve this issue of interpretation, let us review the evidence.

Maimonides's position in the *Mishneh Torah* is
straightforward:

> Freedom of choice (*reshut*) is bestowed on every human
> being. If one desires to turn toward the good way and be
> righteous, he has the power to do so. If one wishes to
> turn toward the evil way and be wicked, he is at liberty
> to do so. "Behold, the man is become as one of us, to
> know good and evil" (Gen. 3:22)—which means that
> the human species has become unique in the world,
> there being no other species like it in the following re-
> spect, namely, that man, of himself and by the exercise of
> his own intelligence and reason, knows what is good
> and what is evil, and there is none who can prevent him
> from doing that which is good or that which is evil.[35]

Similarly, "there is no one that coerces [man] or decrees what
he is to do, or draws him to either of the two ways; but every
person turns to the way which he desires, spontaneously and

of his own volition" (Laws of Repentance 5:2). To Maimonides, this "great principle" (*ikkar gadol*) is the "pillar of the Law and the commandment," without which the rationality of the Torah would collapse.

Elsewhere, though, Maimonides's treatments of this theme are more nuanced. In his *Letter on Astrology*, he denounces astrology as a pseudoscience, distinguishing the fallacious view that the position of the stars at the time of one's birth determines one's character and destiny from the noble, truthful science of astronomy. But then he proceeds to distinguish *both* astrological determinism *and* philosophical indeterminism from the position of the Torah. For Maimonides, as for ibn Gabirol, it seems that the form of our matter predestines us to certain character traits and dispositions. Although it is "impossible for man to be born endowed by nature from his very birth with either virtue or vice," what is in fact possible is that "through natural causes he may from birth be so constituted as to have a *predilection* for a particular virtue or vice."[36] Maimonides leans here on Aristotle, who analyzes virtue and vice as dispositions, partially given in our nature, partially chosen, shaped, and then entrenched in our nature by our choice.[37]

Nonetheless, Maimonides continues to insist, free choice is given. Whether one develops virtuously or viciously remains in our hands, and depending on our choices, a divine calculus of reward and punishment will govern the outcome of our lives. Even though the disconfirming experiences of real life—the suffering of the righteous and well-being of the wicked—force us to admit our ignorance of how divine justice ultimately works, we can attain enough clarity to dispel superstitious nonsense of the kind propagated by the "stargazers" while, at the same time, understand that freedom of choice has to be made compatible with some level of natural and divine determinism.[38]

In *Eight Chapters*, Maimonides interprets the Talmudic dictum we encountered above: "All is in the power of heaven except for the fear of heaven." The "all" here, he notes, is "meant to designate only natural phenomena which are not influenced by the will of man, as whether a person is tall or short, whether it is rainy or dry, whether the air is pure or impure." God has predestined the condition of the physical world from the start: "all things, at all times, are regulated by the laws of nature and run their natural course."[39] But this is different from the idea, embraced by Islamic thinkers yet firmly rejected by Maimonides, that God intervenes moment by moment, event by event. Judaism affirms the integrity of nature as the creation of a good God, and as reflecting stable laws and a general pattern of causality, not the obliteration of nature and natural law altogether.

What is more, even the general pattern of causality seems to stop short at the threshold of the human will. "God created man as a being whose physical nature is such that he can rise and sit down and whose mental nature is such that he has freedom of choice to do so." Or at least that is what Maimonides asserts in *Eight Chapters*. In his *Guide of the Perplexed*, by contrast, he comes close to integrating free choice into natural causality; in the view of some scholars, he actually does so.[40]

Ever since the primordial exercise of divine will at creation—he writes in the *Guide of the Perplexed*—three kinds of
proximate cause are at work: natural, free, and volitional. Natural causes refer to things like snow always melting when the
air becomes warm or waves being stirred when the wind
blows. God does not micromanage nature; expressions in the
Torah where He appears to cause natural effects through com-
manding or speaking should be understood in the sense of His
having established natural laws at the time of creation.

With the second and third kinds of causation, the free and
volitional, the picture becomes more complex. In animals,
Maimonides states, God "arouses" a volition—the desire of a
fish or insect to do something or other—while in rational
human beings He "necessitates" a particular free choice. He
does not do so moment by moment or directly; He has so set
up the world that these processes happen naturally as a chain
of proximate causes. In the words of Shlomo Pines, "In Maimonides' opinion volition and choice are no less subject to
causation than natural phenomena and do not form in this
respect a domain governed by different laws or by no laws
at all."[41]

But what then is the status of free choice? Has Maimonides
not integrated it into the causal matrix of nature, in the process erasing the distinction between irrational animals and
rational humans?[42] If this is Maimonides's true view, then he
is, shockingly, a strict determinist, not at all the voluntarist
who speaks so forthrightly about free will in the other works I
have cited. (There are good reasons to doubt this conclusion.

Maimonides may hold, in Goodman's words, "that all things are determined." But he also holds that "we ourselves are participants in the process of determination."[43] All things are caused, though we, in a robust sense, are among the causes of some of them—principally of our own actions.)

It may then be correct to say that Maimonides moves toward compatibilism, that he believes that whatever the ultimate truth about the scope of causality might be, we need to conceive of ourselves as capable of free choice in order to achieve the moral-intellectual perfection that is possible for us as persons. Perhaps Maimonides wants to balance the rational need for a scientific account of reality against the practical need for a moral-religious life. He wants, that is, to perform Nagel's work of reintegration of a rational scientific conception of ourselves with our felt, personal experience. Maimonides drills down into an ontological domain that is today occupied by neurobiology. Yet he comes back up as well, hanging on to the world in which human persons live. We have seen this tension before in his treatment of the ideal way of life—contemplative or active—at the end of the *Guide of the Perplexed*.

Crescas, the last thinker whom I consider, is more radical than Maimonides. In *The Light of the Lord* (*Or Adonai*), he explores the arguments for free will and determinism, and settles on a strict determinist position. He does so on almost purely philosophical grounds, although broader theological concerns are never absent. While certainly not typical of other Jewish thinkers, Crescas shows how even an extreme stance might be made compatible with the Torah.

In *The Light of the Lord,* Crescas sets up an antinomy between free will and determinism in terms of something whose nature is "possible" and something whose nature is "necessary."[44] By possible, he means contingent—something that presently exists but need not have existed. Its existence is not made necessary by its essence. (For example, the essence of water is that it is H_2O. There is no necessary reason why our universe had to contain water, but given that it does, water must everywhere be H_2O. In this way, both possibility [in the sense of contingency] and necessity coexist.) If the possible is real, if it is a cogent notion, then a metaphysical background would be available for free will. If strict, necessary causality were to govern all things and events, however, then free will would be groundless.

What, then, is the status of free will? Is it something that contingently exists, yet need not, like water, have existed? Arguing that case, Crescas appeals to our experience.[45] We feel that we are able to will or not will that something happen, like moving a limb. If such experiences were compelled or necessary, there could be no experience of free will; everything would collapse into necessity. On the assumption that our experience is veracious, the implication is that possibility is real. Besides, if all were determined, effort and diligence, teaching and learning, would be futile; since we find them valuable, there must be a real point to them. Beyond our own experience, when it comes to the nature of causation as such, Crescas points out that some things have to happen—his example is the rising and setting of the sun—while other things are contingent (like whether I have lemonade in my refrigerator).

From instances of the latter we may conclude that things come about that are *not* necessitated; they are simply possible.

On the side of necessity, Crescas essentially asserts that to admit the very concept of a cause is to admit to the global logic of necessity. All events are effects of long lineages of causation, taking their place in turn as causes of future effects. Until one works back to the first cause (God), all the causal conjunctions have a necessary character; each one has a sufficient antecedent. If something exists that *seems* merely possible (the lemonade), its existence is no less necessitated than something that seems necessary (the sunrise). From this point of view, our experiences are not veracious. Deterministic metaphysics debunks, as it were, folk psychology.

Crescas's discussion is complex and somewhat obscure; I will not review all its moves here. He shifts from logical and causal necessity to theological necessity. He invokes a long-standing theological discussion among Jews, Christians, and Muslims: an omniscient God, who knows all particulars, must know the decisions of human beings in advance. Those decisions therefore cannot, in any real sense, be free.

Crescas himself sides with the determinists. Although from our first-person perspective we feel free to accept or reject a given course of action, the truth is that causal factors determine whether we choose x or not-x. Choice is no more than a feeling of possibility; freedom of the will is a feeling. What distinguishes the will is that it appears as a domain in which we do not *feel* the force of the underlying effective causal factors. There are two perspectives at work: considering things from the inside out, from within the framework of our own experience, the will seems to be free; considering things from another, larger perspective—one that takes a comprehensive view of causality—the will is not free.[46] The individual event of free choice seems contingent—that's how it feels to us—but the broader context in which the event occurs is one of causal necessity.

Crescas thus believes that "the complete truth implied by the Torah and by speculation is that the nature of the possible exists in things with respect to themselves but *not* with respect to their causes. However, publicizing this is dangerous to the masses."[47] Crescas wants to hold both positions in tension— we are not really free, yet the experience of will is a feeling of freedom. So at bottom we are not free, but publicizing this conclusion would be dangerous to the masses, which would take it as an excuse for moral lawlessness. As well they might. But the story does not stop here. Crescas himself found his approach to the problem so inadequate—the problem, in other words, of reconciling philosophical determinism with a theology in which God rewards and punishes people on the basis of their free choices—that he launched a second attempt years later. (*The Light of the Lord* was written over a span of time; the later sections show revisions of earlier ideas.)

In his early approach, we are rewarded or punished for our decisions as well as actions only when they are accompanied by the (illusory) *feeling* that we have decided or acted freely. Yet the causal chains that have led us to perform or violate a divine commandment continue in place, with reward or punishment being the necessary effect. Just as the act of touching fire necessarily burns a person, an individual also is necessarily rewarded or punished by the performance or neglect of mitz-vot.[48] There is an almost-karmic quality here—recompense as natural necessity. Crescas quickly modifies this, claiming that God rewards or punishes only those acts "freely" undertaken, but it is too late: our freedom of choice has already suffered the death of a thousand qualifications.

Years later, Crescas takes a different approach, reminiscent of Frankfurt's. If we perform this mitzvah or violate that one, we are acting out a causal script not of our own making. But we are free to appropriate or repudiate that desire, decision, or action; we are free to feel joy or sadness, approval or remorse. On this view, God's reward or punishment of us does not follow mechanically but instead hinges on our *attitude* toward our desires, decisions, and actions.[49] The experience of desire and joy is the will's pleasure in doing good, during which it enjoys the divine emanation of love. We do seem to have some liberty here at the level of the attitudes we adopt toward our own (less than) voluntary actions.

Crescas's position is difficult, but one can appreciate his problem. He wants to follow science and logic ("speculation"), as he sees them, and wants to uphold a traditional image of the human, with personhood and moral agency as durable realities. That is always the dilemma. His work, like that of the others, shows the sophistication and indeed pathos of the medieval Jewish philosophical mind. But before leaving him, I want to call attention to a small point that can provide a bridge to our modern way of thinking about this problem.

In his early formulation, Crescas makes the commandments into *causes*, and God's reward or punishment of us into *effects*. From our point of view, it is odd to think of a mitzvah as a cause in the same sense that gravity or magnetism is a cause. Medieval Hebrew uses the same word, *sibah*, for what we would denominate as "cause" and "reason." We would separate the two; Hebrew does not distinguish between them. Given a sufficiently rich, in the medieval case, typically Aristotelian analysis of causality, there is a sense to this. Mitzvot can be causes in the sense that they cause us to prosper when we follow them or suffer when we do not. In line with the Aristotelian concept of causation, which includes the idea of teleology—final cause—the mitzvot intend our benefit. Following them "causes" us to realize goodness.

Nonetheless, reducing the phenomena of human decision and choice to purely causal phenomena—neuropsychological processes rather than intentions—seems wrong.[50] This is because much of the debate about free will and determinism turns on whether rational explanation is reducible to causal explanation (and ultimately able to be eliminated), or whether rational explanation can remain intact. Do reasons boil down to causes? Do minds reduce to brains? Can the integrity of our personal point of view prevail or must all the causal arrows point downward, as it were, to physics?

Persons and Reasons

Consider these two statements: the sidewalk is wet because of the rain, and John didn't go to the party because of Sarah. Although the two statements are grammatically almost identical, their underlying logic is quite different. The first is a causal explanation; the second is a rational one. In the first, the rain causes wetness; *a* causes *b*. In the second, we cannot say that Sarah causes John not to attend the party; it's not an "*a* causes *b*" kind of statement. Rather, Sarah has provided John with some *reason* on the basis of which he decided not to attend the party. (The actual reason doesn't matter.)[51]

A rational explanation entails that there are persons, selves, who can deliberate about reasons and then act on the basis of them. To explain what someone has done, one states the reason on the basis of which they acted. One need not talk about neurotransmitters, neuronal firings, acetylcholine, synapses, or anything of the sort. Indeed, to try to explain John's decision at a "deeper" neurobiological level would be weird, at least in the context of a conversation about why he didn't attend the party. If he offered such a "causal" explanation of his absence to Harry, who had invited him to the party, the latter would rightly suspect that John wasn't being straight with him. Such an explanation would be incompatible with John's integrity as a rational and moral agent, as a person and a conscious self who is normally expected to act on the basis of reasons, not causes. What John needs to do in conversation with Harry is to *excuse* himself, not reach into the depths of his brain functioning.[52] And excuse is a moral move, touching on our responsibilities—and lapses—which in turn flow from our status as persons.

We can think of ourselves, when we try to assume a view from nowhere, as nonpersons driven by antecedently sufficient causes rather than as persons motivated by reasons. We can theorize ourselves away. But we cannot avoid having to return to ourselves and continue our lives within a shared form of life in which practices like self-explanation, excuse, and assuming as well as ascribing responsibility remain in force.

From the neurobiological vantage point, the selves to which we return and freedom of choice they seem to enjoy may well be illusions. But if the self or free will is an illusion, it is a deep and peculiar one. It is not the deception of a magician, liar, or philosophical thought experiment. It might, however, be akin to the illusion of a unified visual field. Thus, on the basis of our experience of sight, we might think that our eyes are fixed steadily on some relevant portion of the world. Our eyes in fact move around with astonishing rapidity, stopping, selecting, moving on, and stopping again. These movements, known as saccades, occur in as little as 1/900th of a second. We are not conscious of them. At the conscious level, our visual field is continuous, coherent, and stable.

If, for the sake of argument, we consider that visual coherence and stability are an illusion, then we might have an analogy to free will as an illusion. Our experience of the seamless finished product veils the multiple, discontinuous steps leading up to it.

Visual perception supplies more than an analogy; it offers another example of the difference between experience at the integrated, personal, conscious level and the neurobiological process that precedes as well as enables that experience. The compatibilist will claim that both the neurobiological process and conscious experience cohere, even as the explanations that are requisite to them do different kinds of work. A neuroscientific, causal explanation of John's decision making has its place, and so do his rational explanation and excuse to Harry. To give up on the latter entirely in favor of the former would be to give up on human personhood as a reality.

And that is scarcely intelligible. To unmake a whole world of beliefs and practices, of reason and action, in favor of a world of firings and synapses, nonselves and happenings, requires a decision on our part to substitute one entire frame of reference for another. We would have to agree to cease speaking one way and begin speaking in another one. We would have to decide to undo ourselves. So reductionist a program is not only incoherent; it is absurd.

The Jewish sources I have examined, by stressing the reality of moral persons in a shared world, keep us focused on what is properly expressive of human nature, acting on the basis of reasons rather than by compulsion on the basis of causes. That reasons may themselves be a kind of cause, a position advocated by Hume and Donald Davidson, and anticipated (even linguistically) by medieval philosophers like Maimonides and Crescas, is not fatal to Judaism's stress on moral personhood.

What, then, of the claims of Sellars and Gazzaniga that it is in the shared world, the interactive sphere of persons (or in Gazzaniga's case, multiple brains), that moral concepts such as agency and responsibility arise? These are modern ways of making Locke's point: person is a forensic concept. Persons, no less than citizens, exist in the public realm. In the next chapter, I will consider Judaism's teachings on the social, political, and economic aspects of human nature.

CHAPTER 4
Persons Together

If there is a Jewish version of Aristotle's famous assertion that humans are political animals, it is the saying mentioned by the Talmudic sage Rava: "Either companionship or death" (B. Ta'anit 23a). While not pointing directly to a political form of life, Rava's aphorism does emphasize what underlies politics: the human need for togetherness, the value found in belonging.

The context of the rabbinic saying is a story about another sage, Ḥoni "the Circle-Maker," who lived in Roman Palestine in the first century BCE and had a quasimagical gift for bringing rain to the often-parched land through the power of his prayer. Ḥoni's charisma was also combined with wisdom. In the lead-up to the story, Ḥoni is pondering the meaning of Psalm 126:1, which likens the returnees from the Babylonian exile to dreamers. How, he wonders, was it possible for people to remain in a dreamlike state for seventy years—traditionally, the term of the exile?

His bemusement sets up the narrative. As he walks along a road, Ḥoni sees a man planting a carob tree and asks him how long it will take for the tree to produce fruit. Seventy years, is the reply. Are you confident you will live that long? The man answers: There were carob trees waiting for me when I came into the world; just as my ancestors planted them for me, I am planting them for my descendants.

At this stirring affirmation of family tradition and intergenerational responsibility, Ḥoni sits down to eat and rest. He falls asleep, and while he sleeps, rocks miraculously grow around him, enclosing him within a cave. On awakening, he sees a man gathering fruit from the carob tree. Are you the one who planted it, he asks? No, the man responds, I am his grandson; thus, Ḥoni realizes he has just received a striking answer to his wonderment about enduring dream states.

The story does not end there. Returning to his village, he asks whether Ḥoni's son is still alive. He is told that the son is dead, but the grandson is alive. But I am Ḥoni, he exclaims, to general disbelief. Going to the study hall, he hears the sages say that in the days of Ḥoni, all disputes were resolved because Ḥoni made the law crystal clear. Again he tries to disclose his identity; again no one believes him. Deprived of both credibility and recognition, he prays for death, and his prayer is granted. "Hence the saying," reports Rava later on, "either companionship or death" (*o ḥevruta o mituta*).

In its half-amusing, half-poignant way, the story illustrates the deeply social dimension of human nature. Humans do not need each other generically; they need each other in a highly specific, personal way. As with Adam's need for a companion, unmet by his companionship with the animals, humans need those who are "flesh of my flesh"—not identical with themselves, but like themselves. There must be commonality, a shared world, shared experiences, beliefs, and values. There must be mutual affirmation, respect, and recognition.

Conceivably, Ḥoni might have lived out his days at his grandson's, with food on the table and a roof over his head. Yet he would have been a guest, a stranger, or a charity case—anything but Ḥoni. His would have been a life of survival, not flourishing. In praying to be relieved of such a life, Ḥoni gives expression to the content of a full and satisfying life.

Aristotle would agree. "For without friends no one would choose to live, though he had all other goods" (*Ethics* 1155a5). Friendship is a crucial component of human flourishing (*eudaimonia*), and Aristotle envisions political order as the medium for that flourishing. The polis or city comes into being *after* the bare conditions of existence are satisfied in the family and village—after humans have ceased to live like beasts and have embarked on the road to the fulfillment of their natures. The polis develops naturally from earlier forms of cooperative practice; bees and other gregarious animals naturally cooperate, but human cooperation is of a higher order. Aristotle writes: "For the real difference between man and other animals is that humans alone have perception of good and evil, right and wrong, just and unjust. And *it is the sharing of a common view in these matters that makes a household or a city*" (*Politics* 1253a15).[1]

The Greek political vision is one of virtuous community. The good life consists in the attainment and practice of moral virtues (such as courage and friendship) coupled with intellectual virtues (like practical and philosophical wisdom). The role of the polis is to enable persons to lead this good life together. Happiness in the Aristotelian version is obtained not through withdrawal from the public realm but rather in the midst of it.[2] Short of the dream of a contemplative, god-like existence, politics is the highest form of life for human beings.

Does the Jewish vision invest politics with quite so much significance? Do Jewish sources attend to political life with anything like the fascination of the Greeks? Much of the history related in the Bible concerns political affairs, from the tyranny of pharaonic Egypt to the successes and failures (mostly the failures) of the kings of Israel and Judah. But little interest is shown in politics for its own sake.[3] Politics is a tool or foil for the will of God, an expression of the faithfulness or impiety of Israelite leaders. The political dimension of human life is at best secondary. Primary are fidelity to God along with the pursuit of justice and righteousness.

Nonetheless, the biblical authors believe that some forms of political order are better than others: there is a right and wrong way to exemplify the will of God in political life. The right way is through a kind of compact, a covenant, between rulers and ruled; the wrong way is through force and coercion, with utter disregard for the will of the governed. As much as the Greeks gloried in the significance of politics and founded political science, the Bible's vision of the good life in political society has exercised its own profound effect on Western culture.

The Bible breaks sharply from what we might call the cosmological politics of ancient paganism. The Babylonian creation story, *Enuma Elish*, which in many ways provides the

background for the biblical stories, culminates in the founding of Babylon.[4] The god Marduk creates the city, and then
crowns it with a temple on the artificial mountain that forms
the axis between the realm of the gods and the earthly political realm. In other words, the basic institutions of the polity
are themselves cosmological, part of the order of divine creation. In the Mesopotamian conception, the king, although
not a god, is Marduk's vicegerent and priest, and serves his
needs.

The Bible firmly rejects this idea of divinely authorized
kingship in a polity founded by a god during the act of creation.[5] The creation narrative of Genesis 1 does not culminate
in the founding of a city-state. It culminates in a pair of human
beings who know no political community and a God who,
resting from His labors, tells human beings to do the same.
The institution founded in creation is not the state but instead
the Sabbath. Politics comes afterward, as an expression of
human experimentation, discovery, and initiative.

True, a dim echo of cosmological-political order may be
found in God's appointment of the sun and moon to rule the
day and night, to dominate and divide time (Gen. 1:18). The
cosmos itself is thus given a quasipolitical shape, with God as
its sovereign head. But this politically inflected cosmos is not
the warrant for later human political rule. That will be based
on popular consent as well as divine approval.

The earliest experiment with politics to which the Bible
gives a fleeting mention is the cryptic reference to Nimrod
(Gen. 10: 8–10)—the first human being to whom rulership is
attributed. The verses referring to him as a king are in the so-

called Table of Nations, a formulaic list of Noah's descendants. The list is an early example of ethnography in which peoples, traditionally numbered seventy, are grouped first in clans (*mishpaḥot*), and then by nations (*goyim*) distinguished by linguistic and territorial commonality. To this otherwise-natural process Nimrod is credited with giving a specifically political accent:

> Cush also begot Nimrod, who was the first man of might on earth.
> He was a mighty hunter by the grace of the Lord; hence the saying, "Like Nimrod a mighty hunter by the grace of the Lord."
> The mainstays of his kingdom were Babylon, Erech, Accad, and Calneh in the land of Shinar.

The ascription of hunting prowess to Nimrod signals a Mesopotamian royal trait that would have been well known to an Israelite audience, while the "saying" about him was likely a form of idiomatic expression in the ancient Near East. Note that it is Nimrod, not Marduk, who founds the city of Babylon and others that were the mainstays or, more literally, beginnings of his kingdom. Although the text is not overtly negative about the origins of human political order, a hint of negative evaluation lurks in Nimrod's name. It may derive from the root *m-r-d*, indicating rebellion, or from *r-d-h*, indicating oppressive rule.

Picking up this scent, rabbinic midrash and later commentators turn Nimrod into a tyrant who deceives humans to secure their consent, builds the Tower of Babel, establishes a state religion of idolatry, and tortures his dissenting subject, Abraham, when the latter challenges his malign theopolitical cult.[6] Interpretations such as these emphasize the cunning of Nimrod and credulity of the people who followed him. The implication is that just rule, by contrast, is based on legitimate consent. This principle is amplified later in the Bible in the dramatic request of the Israelites for a king.

In the centuries between the near-direct rule of God, mediated by his prophet Moses, and establishment of dynastic kingship in Israel, temporary rulers (*shoftim*, or judges) arose to unite the disparate tribes in times of need. This form of intermittent, charismatic authority best preserved the immediate rule of God as sovereign—but at the cost of a sustained or stable national order. Except for the occasional judges, the Israelite experience was one of local and tribal rule. When Samuel, the last of the judges, grew old, an assembly of local chieftains (*zekenim*, or elders) came to him. They demanded a king to rule over them, as Samuel's sons were unfit to rule in the traditional adventitious manner. The elders wanted a king "like all the other nations" (I Sam. 8:5). Deeply chagrined, Samuel prays to God for guidance. God's reply is stern:

> Heed the demand of the people in everything they say to you. For it is not you that they have rejected; *it is Me they have rejected as their king.* Like everything else they have done ever since I brought them out of Egypt to this day—forsaking Me and worshipping other gods— so are they doing to you. Heed their demand; but warn

them solemnly, and tell them about the practices of any king who will rule over them. (I Sam. 8:7–9; emphasis added)

Samuel duly proceeds to describe to the people what a monarchy will be like. Their decision, he tells them, will trigger an upward spiral of land expropriation, taxation, support for a standing army, ever-increasing need for personnel and matériel; the people will lose their sons, daughters, slaves, livestock, and land as the royal house appropriates more and more to sustain itself as well as prosecute its military campaigns. Undeterred, the people persist: "We must have a king to rule over us, that we may be like all the other nations; let our king rule over us and go out at our head and fight our battles" (I Sam. 8:19–20).

Later Jewish exegetes had to reconcile the broadly antipolitical thrust of this tradition with other texts endorsing the eventual monarchy. Deuteronomy 17:14–20 affirms the decision to appoint a king, albeit contingently: "If, after you have entered the land, . . . you decide that 'I will set a king over me, as do all the nations about me,' you shall be free to set a king over yourself, one chosen by the Lord your God." It is not immediately clear whether this is a commandment or grant of permission. In any case, Deuteronomy then goes on to limit the king's powers, mitigate any tendency toward absolutism, and make the king mindful of his duties to God. But there is no mention here and no historical evidence of any mechanism, short of divine intervention, for curbing royal power.[7] In fact, the full acceptance of the monarchy is indicated by several royal psalms, which liken the Davidic ruler to God's son.

Given this, we seem to have an initial resistance to political rule by anyone other than God. The preferred form of rule is theocracy, to use the term coined by Flavius Josephus. With time, this extreme skepticism about human political rule is tempered until, in Mesopotamian style, the king becomes the vicegerent of God and a cosmological element enters into the justification of Israelite political institutions. But then, with the eventual loss of self-rule and collapse of the Davidic monarchy, political organization among the Jews, to the degree that it persists, acquires a more humble justification. The old covenantal theme of legitimacy through consent becomes the norm for Jewish communities throughout history. The self-governing Jewish communities of the Middle Ages and early modernity were republican in nature. They were based on an agreement between persons to live together in community, under the protection—when the Jews were fortunate—of gentile rulers who left them alone (as long as they paid their taxes) to manage their own affairs.

The point is that the rule of some human beings over others has legitimacy when it does not subvert, replace, or challenge the rule of God over human beings. When it actually augments the rule of God, as in the deferred Davidic kingship of the messianic age, politics reaches the apogee of its significance. Until then, however, political life is balanced on a razor's edge of too much or too little. The polity that Nimrod sought to found is an example of too much—a state so strong that it would rival God.

Although the connection is not made in the Bible, the rabbis, as I have mentioned, attributed to Nimrod the impetus for building the Tower of Babel. Humanity had been united—"everyone on earth had the same language and the same words"—yet people feared they would be "scattered all over the world" (Gen. 11:1, 4). Perhaps the experience of migration from the east (Gen. 11:2) had suggested to them the impermanence of human settlement or indeed the deeper impermanence of human existence. Their solution was to found a city—an ordered political society—with a tower in its midst. The tower would reach to the sky—that is, it would infringe on or penetrate the divine realm. Through the great tower, the people would "make a name" for themselves (Gen. 11:4) and secure their endurance through the ravages of time.

The city founders and tower builders have legitimate concerns, based in deep human needs, but the Bible construes them as occasions of rebellion against God, who is evidently threatened by concerted human action on a global scale.[8] Evoking the primordial rebellion of Adam and Eve in the garden, God says, "If, as one people with one language for all, this is how they have begun to act, then nothing that they may propose to do will be out of their reach. Let us, then, go down and confound their speech there, so that they shall not understand one another's speech" (Gen. 11:6–7).

Just as Adam and Eve were exiled to prevent their further infringement on divine prerogatives (Gen. 3:22), the "generation of the dispersal," as the rabbis call it, was divided into separate nations and linguistic groupings, permanently delimiting the extent of human cooperation.

One would have thought that a united, cooperative humanity was a good thing. But God's rejection of the project implies that human unity has value only insofar as its ends are just. The tower builders, on the biblical and rabbinic view, have sought to replace God, intending to set up an idol with a sword in its hand at the top of the tower (Genesis Rabba 38:6). The eventual though still partial reunification of humanity in the messianic age will come about when God is recognized as the true ruler of all. Until then, the norm will be division into peoples, nations, territories, and languages, with all the possibilities for misunderstanding and conflict thereby entailed.

The Tower of Babel is a mordant comment on the hubris of Mesopotamian civilization. To the Bible, Babylon is a scene of chaos, leading God to confuse (*balal*) the languages of humans and sow enduring division into the human condition. The rabbinic response to this divided condition is neither a lament nor celebration of the ensuing diversity. It is an attempt to legislate a fundamental body of law, equivalent to natural law in the Roman and Christian traditions, that will supply a ground floor of legitimacy to every human moral and political community that observes it.

The rabbis fill out the covenant between God and Noah (Gen. 9:8–11) with seven commandments: to refrain from blasphemy, idolatry, adultery, bloodshed, robbery, and eating the flesh of a living animal, and—a positive commandment—establish courts of justice.[9] Non-Jews have "a portion of the world to come" on the basis of their compliance with Noahide law; they need not become Jews. The Noahide laws do not stipulate what kind of political regime is proper; by implication, any regime that maintains courts capable of equity and justice will fulfill the divine expectation for humanity. For early modern thinkers like Hugo Grotius and John Selden, the Noahide commandments became a precedent in their development of international law. The commandments stipulate the minimal conditions for human flourishing within a just political order. They—and natural law sensibility that lies behind them—articulate the universal moral norms requisite to the dignity, protection, and worth of persons.

If Babel indicates the expectation of too much from politics, the chaotic circumstances of premonarchical Israel indicate too little attention paid to securing stable communal life through political means. The direct rule of God—which is to say, the underdevelopment of central political institutions—fails to preserve order, justice, and liberty among the Israelites. The Book of Judges depicts a recurrent and worsening deterioration in relations among the Israelite tribes as well as between them and the surrounding gentile populations. The indictment of the text is that as there was no king, "every man did what was right in his own eyes."

This tendency toward lawlessness is given its most tragic expression in the horrific story of the concubine of Gibeah (Judges, chapter 19), with which the Book of Judges culminates.[10] A traveler from Ephraim stops in the Benjaminite town of Gibeah, where he is met by an elderly resident who begs him to enter his home and not sleep in the street. After the traveler and his concubine enjoy the man's hospitality, the brutish residents of the town pound on the elderly man's door demanding that the visitor come forth so that they can rape him. (There is an allusion here to the earlier story of Lot, his angelic visitors, and the evil men of Sodom.) The man pleads with his neighbors to desist, offering his own daughter and the visitor's concubine instead. At length, the concubine is sent out. Gang raped through the night, she dies on the doorstep at first light.

The Ephraimite traveler—who has hardly distinguished himself for chivalry—returns home with the woman's corpse, which he cuts into twelve pieces, sending a piece to each tribe with a demand for vengeance. A civil war ensues as the Benjaminites refuse to hand over the men from Gibeah who committed the outrage. In the end, the tribe of Benjamin—men, women, and children—is almost entirely wiped out. Such are the depraved depths to which the Israelites sank when "everyone did as he pleased" (Judges 21:25).

The anointment of Saul, the first king—his background as a Benjaminite provides a narrative link to the story just told—is meant to restore balance: to introduce a stable, national political institution that will allow the tribes to work in concert and mitigate the possibility of further civil war. But Saul's elevation and reign are a less than successful experiment in establishing a new kind of regime—though an experiment that also reveals the elements of a proper politics in the eyes of the biblical historian. God has instructed the prophet Samuel to heed the people's request for a king, but also "warn them solemnly" about the inevitable consequences and excesses of kingship; the people have to know just what they are agreeing to. Legitimate rule, in other words, requires *both* approval by God *and* the consent of the people. The relevant factors are all evident in I Samuel, chapter 10. After God has chosen Saul, and Samuel has anointed him, Samuel shows Saul to the people, who "acclaimed him, shouting, 'Long live the king!'" (I Sam. 10:24).

Tragically, Saul proves to be a failure: petty, vainglorious, and disobedient of God's commands. After his ignominious defeat by the Philistines and suicide on Mount Gilboa, the pattern of selection and investiture is repeated with David. Favored by God to rule after the disfavored Saul, David is appointed by the men of Judah as their tribal commander (II Sam. 2:4), and then following his successful campaign against the remaining loyalists of Saul, elected as king of all Israel in a public assembly at Hebron. Once the people have acknowledged David's beneficence toward them in war and his selection by God, the elders, who represent the remaining political institution of the day, enter into a covenant with him and anoint him king.

The term *berit*, "covenant," is crucial. The relationship between God and the people, initiated at Sinai, is a berit (Exod. 19:5), and so too is this purely intrahuman relationship between ruler and ruled. (Subsequently, God Himself enters into a berit with David.) As the typical biblical way of establishing a political relationship, covenanting relies on human memory, discernment, evaluation, and choice. The covenantal partners recall their prior relationship, typically in terms of the beneficence that one party has shown the other—as in the historical prologue to the Decalogue, in which God recalls for his imminent human partners His past action on Israel's behalf (Exod. 20:2). The benefited partners discern a proper response to the beneficent One, such as gratitude or loyalty, and evaluate the future benefits to be gained as well as the possible costs to be incurred; the covenant with God recorded in Deuteronomy 27–28 includes a warning as to the dreadful consequences of violation. Finally, they publicly pledge themselves to fealty and fidelity: "Moses went and repeated to the people all the commands of the Lord and all the rules; and all the people answered with one voice, saying, 'All the things that the Lord has commanded we will do!' Moses then wrote down all the commands of the Lord" (Exod. 24:3).

Consent is as central an element of the biblical political vision as it is in the social contract tradition, which drew on biblical covenantal thought for its inspiration.[11] A proper politics is not built on conquest, natural organic development, or divine fiat. It requires the approval of those who will be governed. A legitimate polity is one where the dignity of those who comprise it must be secure and where the capacity for judgment must be given expression. A biblical and Jewish vision of a good politics respects the personhood of those who form the polity.

One might object that once the will of God is introduced, consent cannot get a foothold. How much freedom do human beings have to choose once God has already made His choice? Nor are such questions peculiar to a theological context; they apply to the nature of consent in general. Within the social contract tradition, for example, the question quickly arises as to how the consent of a founding generation, which emerges from the state of nature, can bind subsequent ones. Involved here are the limits of the very concept of consent itself. The upshot is that consent is necessary but not sufficient to secure a proper politics. Consent is crucial, yet it is not the only thing that is crucial. Also making for political stability are force, habit, need, inertia, and other factors that do not have the moral value implicit in consent. The need for these introduces moral ambiguity into politics. Political order is necessary for human flourishing, given the innate sociality of humans. But political order, notwithstanding its justice, can, even at its best, offend against moral norms.

What is remarkable in the Jewish tradition is that consent plays as large a role as it does. In a famous midrash, God holds Mount Sinai over the heads of the people and informs them that if they don't "consent" to enter a covenant with Him, the mountain will be dropped on their heads. The rabbis comment that this scenario would offer a powerful objection to the Torah—namely, that it was imposed by force. They conclude that in the days of Mordecai and Esther, many years after Sinai, the Jews freely consented to take the commandments on themselves and affirm the terms of the covenant (B. Shabbat 88a).[12] Indeed, ceremonies of covenant renewal in biblical times (for instance, Joshua 24) or ritual ratifications of the covenant continued to characterize Jewish life.[13] The Jewish vision of politics sees the denizens of the polity actively engaged in work for the common good (*tovat ha-klal*), jointly sustaining the conditions under which persons, in the Judaic version of flourishing, may lead godly lives. Political order may begin in the evolutionary adaptations of social primates, but in its human form it emerges in the decisions of persons to augment a common good.

Wealth and Property

The Jews did not make politics as conceptually thematic to the fulfillment of human nature, to the attainment of eudaimonia, as did the Greeks. Nevertheless, living in a legitimate political community is a great boon to human flourishing, to the life of Torah, and living without it is a great impediment. "If not for the fear of the government," the rabbis comment, "men would eat one another alive" (Avot 3:2)—not exactly an encomium to political life, but not a dismissal of its importance either. More positively, the tradition embraces the teaching of the prophet Jeremiah: "Seek the welfare of the city to which I have exiled you and pray to the Lord in its behalf; for in its prosperity you shall prosper" (Jer. 29:7).

This leads us to another set of questions at the core of human togetherness: In what does Jeremiah's "prosperity" (*shalom*) consist? What role does material well-being play in human flourishing? How do prosperity, market relations, labor, and leisure express and protect human dignity?

Aristotle distinguishes sharply between the domestic sphere (*oikos*) and public realm (polis). Economics is a sphere without freedom, a domain of master and slaves, of paterfamilias, and wife and children. It is a place of terminally unequal persons. Politics, by comparison, is a realm of free and equal men. The underlying assumption is that work is menial; although some forms of labor are more virtuous than others, none of them rises to the dignity of the free man in the public sphere. Politics—engagement in virtuous public life—is possible only for men of property and a certain amount of wealth, for men of leisure.

Wealth, for Aristotle, is to be found primarily in land, livestock, and the produce of nature; not an end in itself, it is rather a means to the end of leisure. Moneymaking, by contrast, is the acquisition of wealth for its own sake. When the goods of nature are no longer grown, raised, or bartered, but given market value and traded through a means of exchange, then human beings have taken a step beyond nature, and the way is open to a perverse inversion of ends and means.[14] Acquisitiveness—getting more than nature requires, and making money with money by lending at interest—are marks of such perversity.

Aristotle's view of wealth meshed well with the ascetic strain of medieval Christianity, but the capitalist societies emerging in early modern Protestant lands turned against Aristotelian economic thought as they turned against Rome. For Aristotle, property is a mere entry condition for public life; for Locke, property is *the* value that public life—that is, the state established through the social contract—intends to protect. Human beings in the "state of nature" choose to give over some of their rights to a sovereign precisely because, in their prepolitical position, they are unable to secure their right to their property adequately. The public realm is a means to safeguard the inalienable rights of life, liberty, and property, and serve the private sphere, where the satisfactions of life are largely found. Politics is the scaffolding that surrounds the productive, wealth-developing project of Lockean humans.

For Aristotle, nature (and hence human nature) decrees a norm of sufficiency—enough but not more. For Locke, nature is inherently insufficient; human activity, which domesticates nature to our purposes and creates property, perfects nature. The more work, the better.

Jewish thought has elements of both views. To begin with, labor is not the sorry fate of humanity after its expulsion from the garden. While still in Eden, Adam was told to "till [the earth] and tend it" (Gen. 2:15). After the expulsion, labor becomes difficult—"by the sweat of your brow shall you get bread to eat" (Gen. 3:19)—but is not in itself ignoble.[15] The central blessings of the biblical vision—a land "flowing with milk and honey," fertile crops and herds, rain in its season, children, and the length of days—assume the productive labor of human beings adding value to the gifts of created nature. Both Eden and its aftermath require tilling and tending. As covenantal partners of God, human beings must cultivate the natural world in which God has placed them. Taking responsibility for the created world is part of what it means for human beings to be created in the image of God.[16]

Exercising that responsibility implies *skilled* labor. The Talmud observes that whoever does not teach their child a trade teaches them to be a thief (B. Kiddushin 29a). A gambler, who doesn't have a regular profession and isn't involved in advancing the "settlement of the world" through his labor, is barred from acting as a legal witness (B. Sanhedrin 24b). Jewish sources are generally effusive in their praise of work: if one has to, one should flay a carcass in the street—the meanest profession imaginable—rather than declare that such work is beneath one (B. Pesaḥim 113a). Rabban Gamliel taught that the study of Torah must be combined with a worldly occupation and that study alone, without a life of work, will not stand (Avot 2:2).

Yet labor must not dominate life. Being created in the image of God also requires that human beings cease from their creative labor, as God ceased from His:

> Remember the Sabbath day and keep it holy. Six days you shall labor and do all your work, but the seventh day is a Sabbath of the Lord your God; you shall not do any work—you, your son or daughter, your male or female slave, or your cattle, or the stranger who is within your settlements. For in six days the Lord made heaven and earth and sea, and all that is in them, and He rested on the seventh day; therefore the Lord blessed the Sabbath day and hallowed it. (Exod. 20:8–11)

The value of work is relative to a set of higher values. The Sabbath is not about rest as such; it is about refraining from work, defined as creative activity that transforms nature for the sake of human ends.[17] The essentially creative nature of work emulates the creative impulse of divine work; to refrain from work is to let creation return to its Creator. It is also to let human beings step out of their identity as producers and return for a day to their identity as persons created in the image of God. It is in light of the latter identity that the former finds its value.

Jewish economic thought gives rather free rein to private property, competition, trade, investment, and the acquisition of wealth—far more so than did medieval Christianity. But it does not trust entirely in the invisible hand of the market. Nor, for that matter, did Adam Smith (1723–90), the philosopher of political economy who insisted that self-interest be moderated by the sentiment of benevolence to ensure basic justice. And moral self-command was not enough; Smith also relied on government to guarantee that market actors played fair.

Rabbinic Judaism has all these traits. There are laws governing economic activity, values regarding economic life inculcated by the Torah, and a history in Jewish self-governing communities of rabbinic intervention in markets to ensure fairness.[18]

As in Locke, Judaism gives private property a secure place. "In contrast to the classical Christian view," writes Isaac Lifshitz, "in which ownership is conditional and relates to the manner of an object's use and the owner's vocation and responsibilities, the right to private property in Judaism is nearly absolute and can be restricted only in the most extreme circumstances."[19] The earth is the Lord's, but the Lord gives responsibility for it—indeed, dominion over it—to human beings. Acquiring property through labor and securing possession through legal means are sacrosanct. Numerous commandments prohibit stealing, fraud, invasion, or abuse of another's property; all attest to the significance of ownership.

An acute instance is Deuteronomy 22:1:

If you see your fellow's ox or sheep gone astray, do not ignore it; you must take it back to your fellow. If your fellow does not live near you or you do not know who he is, you shall bring it home and it shall remain with you until your fellow claims it; then you shall give it back to him. You shall do the same with his ass; you shall do the same with his garment; and so too shall you do with anything that your fellow loses and you find; you must not remain indifferent.

One has a moral and legal duty to restore another's property. One cannot say "it is not my problem; it's their problem." Indifference is not allowed. Property rights are paramount, even if one is inconvenienced. Respect for the property rights of others entails that one cannot even inwardly desire a takeover of another's property, let alone make an outward move to seize it. The last commandment of the Decalogue (Exod. 19:14; Deut. 5:18) proscribes coveting "anything that is your neighbor's," and Jewish tradition takes this to encompass both envious thought and practical steps to induce someone to give up or sell the coveted property.

The right to property legitimately acquired implies that no one has a *right* to another's property; it is for the owner to do with—to retain, sell, transfer, or even destroy—as they wish.[20] Private property, an occasion to exercise responsibility for a portion of the world, enhances the agency and dignity of the person who controls it.

But what of the poor, who don't have sufficient property for their needs and well-being? What of *their* dignity? It is well known that historically, Jewish communities maintained comprehensive welfare systems, and Jews today continue such practices on a voluntary basis. In fact, sharing one's wealth with those in need is a religious duty (*tzedakah*).

Still, those in need do not, strictly speaking, have a *right* to one's property. Locke's view that the surplus of one's wealth must be given to the poor reflects centuries of Christian teaching.[21] Judaism, with its emphasis on private property, approaches the problem of poverty differently. The promise in Deuteronomy 15:4, "There shall be no needy among you," is understood to entail an obligation to prevent *oneself* from becoming poor.[22] Poverty demeans human dignity and constrains the poor from caring for the world. The biblical and Jewish approach to poverty is aimed, above all, at restoring dignity by enhancing responsibility.

The Bible provides the basis for the duty of tzedakah. Among the many agricultural laws, several provide for the landless poor. Thus, in the so-called Holiness Code (Lev. 19), we read: "When you reap the harvest of your land, you shall not reap all the way to the edges of your field or gather the gleanings of your harvest. You shall not pick your vineyard bare, or gather the fallen fruit of your vineyard; you shall leave them for the poor and the stranger: I the Lord am your God." In Deuteronomy's (24:19) version of this same commandment, an additional case is covered: "When you reap . . . and overlook a sheaf in the field, do not turn back to get it; it shall go to the stranger; the fatherless, and the widow— in order that the Lord your God may bless you in all your undertakings."

These five categories—the unharvested grain at the corner of the field, the harvested grain that has been left behind, fruits still remaining on the trees, fruits fallen from trees, and forgotten produce—are extensively developed in rabbinic law, complete with definitions of terms and measures as well as the laying out of symmetrical obligations for farmers and impoverished gleaners alike. Jewish law fixes the area of the unharvested grain (*peah*) at a minimum of one-sixtieth of the field (though the farmer has to leave more if the field is small or if in a given year the poor are many); the area must be clearly demarcated; the farmer must be allowed to finish his work before the poor can enter his property; and the peah has to remain in the ground so that the gleaners must engage in agricultural labor themselves. Farmers are permitted to harvest three times per day, at hours set aside so as to accommodate different types of people (nursing mothers, young children, the elderly, etc.). If the farmer forgets to leave peah, he has to give away its equivalent to the poor or face corporal punishment.

And so on for the other categories that the farmer is obligated to leave annually (in addition to a fixed tithe on produce to be given to the poor in the third and sixth years of the sabbatical cycle).[23] In principle, all these rules are still binding on Jewish farmers, both within and outside the Land of Israel.

Another source for tzedakah derives from Deuteronomy 15:7–8 and its parallel in Leviticus 25:35: "If, however, there is a needy person among you, one of your kinsmen in any of your settlements in the land that the Lord your God is giving you, do not harden your heart and shut your hand against your needy kinsman. Rather, you shall assuredly open your hand and lend him sufficient for whatever he needs."

This text establishes both a positive commandment to give charity and negative commandment not to resent the poor—from which a third-century rabbinic commentary, the *Sifre*, draws out implications that remain normative in the Talmud and later codes.[24] In its view, the opening references to a "needy person," "your kinsmen," "your settlements," and "the land" establish an order of priority. The neediest have the greatest claim on charitable resources. The inhabitants of your own city take precedence over those people elsewhere, as do the inhabitants of Israel over those outside its borders. Rabbinic Judaism, unlike Kantian ethics, does legitimate the natural human impulse to favor one's own, those closest to one, before favoring others. This is not, of course, absolute. But the tradition does acknowledge, as we see here, that there is a hierarchy of caring. Those closest to us, in whom we have invested the most care and concern, are properly served first.

The repetition of a verb form (*patoah tiphtah*, you shall assuredly open [your hand]), which in biblical grammar functions to provide emphasis, is taken to signify both that one must offer charity repeatedly and, if the offer is declined (perhaps because it is embarrassing), then offer the gift as a loan. As to what constitutes "sufficient" support, one need not make the recipient rich, but one must replicate the standard of living to which that person was accustomed before his or her impoverishment. As an example, the text cites the sage Hillel who "gave a certain poor man from a noble family a horse to exercise and a slave to wait on him. On another occasion in Upper Galilee a guest was served a pound of meat every day."[25]

With the transition in Hellenistic times from an agricultural to urban economy, rabbinic Jews created a system whereby the community itself facilitates the provision of welfare. Here is Maimonides's summary statement:

> Every city that has Jews is obligated to appoint officials who are well known and trustworthy, who will go among the people during the weekdays and collect from each one what is appropriate and what has been assessed of him. Then they will distribute a weekly ration of food. We have never seen or heard of a Jewish community that does not have such a fund for charity. . . . In [some communities], the officials collect each day from every courtyard bread and food and fruit or money. They then distribute to the poor their daily needs.[26]

The communal provision of welfare does not exempt an individual from the religious duty of tzedakah, though. Responsibility for one's portion of the world implies responsibility to the poor in one's family, one's community, and beyond. This is both duty and virtue in the sense that one who cares about lifting up the poor emulates God's attributes of love and compassion. The communal provision of support is an expression of the aspiration of the community for holiness, for collective emulation of the divine. If charitable giving is virtuous, selfish refusal to give, especially when there is no harm suffered in giving, is vicious. The rabbis speak of compelling people, who would otherwise act badly, to behave properly (just as a recalcitrant husband can be coerced by the court until he gives a divorce "willingly").

The emphasis throughout is on the personal responsibility of giver *and* receiver. Legal definitions of poverty and means tests existed to determine the extent of communal obligations to poor persons. Living off welfare, so to speak, was never intended to become a way of life. Along with the requirements for tact and delicacy in questioning applicants so as not to cause shame, there is the intent to motivate them to work their way out of poverty.

According to a well-known Mishnah, "One who says, 'My property is mine and yours is yours,' is an average character type, but some say this [attitude] is the characteristic of Sodom" (Avot 5:13). The ambiguity is interesting. From the perspective of the law, which takes the average person as its measure, "mine is mine and yours is yours" is an acceptable criterion. From the vantage point of the virtuous aspiration of a holy community, it is radically insufficient. Property rights are not infringed; law and community must respect the rights of ownership. But one made in the image of God should strive for something higher.

Jewish sources are in agreement with Aristotle that sociality is fundamental to humans. Unlike in the picture painted by Hobbes or Rousseau, human beings in the Jewish perspective are communal by nature—primordially interdependent. But there is also a Lockean element: political arrangements at their best are neither organic, on the one hand, nor imposed, on the other; they are deliberated on and chosen, and serve to protect the interests of the persons who choose them. One of those interests is property. The community must care for its most impoverished members, but must do so while respecting the property of individuals.

Sociality, Individuality, and Evolution

If the Western tradition of political and social thought is divided, as Pinker maintains, between thinkers who give primacy to community (the "sociological tradition") and those who give primacy to the individual (the "economic tradition"), Judaism manages to synthesize both.[27] Our sociality gives independent reality to families, tribes, peoples, and nations. Our personhood, however, implies that we can achieve some critical distance from the social contexts that seem natural to us, but that can also be regarded as artifacts and institutions, products of human agency. The clearest example of this in Jewish thought is the Bible's attitude toward the people of Israel as such—a phenomenon that reflects both "kinship and consent" (in the phrase of Daniel J. Elazar). The people of Israel is familial *and* contractual, an organic core descended from biological patriarchs and what Max Weber calls an "oath-bound confederation" founded at Mount Sinai.[28] With kinship and consent in play, Jewish sources reflect a view of human nature that prizes both sociality and individuality.

Contemporary students of human nature along with the moral, political, and economic relations that flow from it look to the behavior of our primate cousins, the great apes, for clues to the evolution of our own social practices. Altruism toward kin, for instance, which often expands to nonkin (so-called reciprocal altruism), appears to be grounded in prehuman emotional responses. Is "ethics," then, just our name for what some of the great apes are already doing among themselves? Is a polity a culturally evolved version of a hominid band evident among a troop of chimpanzees? Is an economy an outgrowth of practices evident wherever reciprocal altruism occurs in primate species?

Aristotle, ever the biologist, notices the similarity between humans and other gregarious species. But he marks a sharp difference in humanity's "perception of good and evil" and the capacity for language with which to articulate that perception. Modern scientific and philosophical advocates of a strong continuity between ape and human "morality" demur. Of course, they concede, human moral practices are more developed and self-conscious, but they come from the same place: the emotional inclination of benevolence, as Smith would have called it, or altruism. "The evolutionary origin of this inclination," primatologist Frans de Waal observes, "is no mystery. All species that rely on cooperation—from elephants to wolves and people—show group loyalty and helping tendencies."[29]

De Waal describes a process whereby an automatic neurological response, emotional contagion, is developed into empathy. Rhesus monkeys, in his illustration, "refuse to pull a chain that delivers food to themselves if doing so shocks a companion. One monkey stopped pulling a chain for five days, and another one for twelve days after witnessing shock delivery to a companion. . . . Such sacrifice relates to the tight social system and emotional linkage among these macaques."[30] Of course, the monkeys are not trying to be good; they are acting according to their nature, following a script evolved over hundreds of thousands of years to maximize their individual and collective survival. If human morality constitutes a break from this lengthy evolutionary prehistory, de Waal would argue, it is only because we can reflect consciously on our dispositions and inclinations, make choices among them, engage in linguistic practices such as justifying or criticizing our behaviors, and so on. That is simply *our* way of being social animals. But are persons reducible to social animals? Does this evolutionary causal explanation subvert the kind of rational explanation that gives support to our personhood?

Suppose we could determine that human morality indeed evolved from the behaviors of our hominid ancestors, and simply constitutes the "best practices" of cooperative primates driven by their genes to replicate, reproduce, and survive. If you accept a story like that as true, would it help you to make a moral decision? Can you get from an explanatory, causal story to a moral judgment? Not easily. You could use the story as a piece of a moral argument, although such reasoning would stand or fall not on its scientific but rather its moral merits. As we noted in the first chapter (in discussing Nagel's ideas), if a Freudian, Marxist, or Nietzschean were to challenge Jewish, Christian, or bourgeois ethics as just so much oedipal sublimation, false consciousness, or *resentment*, no one need feel obliged to abandon their ethics unless a better ethics—not a "scientific" explanation—were offered. And that better ethics would need to be backed up by a moral claim for its superiority.

In short, the sphere of ethics, of arguing about values, rules, judgments, actions, virtues, vices, and so on, retains its integrity no matter what explanatory story is proffered to account for it. But this is not to say that ethics floats freely high above our nature as evolved, biological creatures. The most compelling values, practices, and rules are those that suit our nature, or at least its better angels. As many of our sources have contended, one salient dimension of our nature is to be capable of critical distance from ourselves as natural beings. As conscious persons, we are self-transcending; we are not zombies. We are not just going through the motions of some foreordained genetic program. We know ourselves to be peculiar creatures in the world, self-aware and self-conscious to an extraordinary, biologically unprecedented degree. Putting it dramatically, the political theorist George Kateb remarks that "all other species are more alike than humanity is like any of them; a chimpanzee is more like an earthworm than a human being, despite the close biological relation of chimpanzees to human beings." Though the genetic difference is small, the difference in potential for what we may become is incalculably large. "Only the human species," Kateb concludes, "is, in the most important existential respects, a break with nature and significantly not natural."[31] This seems to me an overstatement, but it nonetheless limns a truth.

The turning back of consciousness onto itself, enabling an ever-greater sense of distance toward both our sensory engagement with the world and our own standing within it, underwrites the distinctiveness of the human. Ethics flows from *both* the dispositions we have evolved as biological creatures to cooperate and thus to survive, *and* conscious reflection on those dispositions. Ethics is both a product of evolution and cultural coevolution, which is driven by persons in their social togetherness and cultural creativity.

This is evident in the case of violence—that abiding and spectacular failure of human togetherness. Groups of chimpanzees show what de Waal calls "community concern": "In apes, we can see the beginnings of this when they smooth relations between others. Females may bring males together after a fight between them, thus brokering a reconciliation, and high-ranking males often stop fights among others in an even-handed manner, thus promoting peace in the group." Apes have a stake, as do humans, in more than their own individual or their kin's survival; they have a stake in the survival of their group. Social pressure works to both encourage group-promoting behavior and discourage group-undermining behavior.[32] And nothing enhances the solidarity of one's own group more than hostility toward outside groups; political philosopher Carl Schmitt is not entirely wrong to see the distinction between friend and foe as the basis of political order.[33] As de Waal puts it, "The profound irony is that our noblest achievement—morality—has evolutionary ties to our basest behavior—warfare. The sense of community required by the former was provided by the latter."[34]

If our evolved hominid nature drives us to regard outsiders with suspicion and hostility, as creatures who are not like us, is it then futile to hope for something like what Kant called "perpetual peace"? Is human social and political life at its best just the (temporary) absence of conflict—conflict suppressed by force? Is the Jewish messianic hope for a peaceable kingdom—not a cessation of conflict, but instead a wholeness or perfection of our nature—a feckless dream? If traits evolved in Africa hundreds of thousands of years ago are our destiny, then Niccolò Machiavelli and Hobbes got it right, and Moses got it wrong. Ours would be a case where the moral imagination must sober up and constrain itself to, at best, the outer limits of our shabby natures.

But if the Jewish tradition shows us anything, it is that we act in conformity with our nature when we elevate, improve, and sanctify it. Here is one homely example: when Jews engage in the most basic biological act of eating, they bless the bread and see it imaginatively as brought forth from the earth by God. That is to say, the culturally evolved practices of agriculture, cooking, and baking, the actions of human beings who add value to the endowments of nature, are godly. As co-creators of the world with God, we are not just the sport of our biochemistry. We are persons who can select and choose among the traits that comprise our very own natures, cultivating some and weeding out others. We cannot ignore what evolutionary biology has made of us, but neither are we exempt from the duty to improve on it.

Conclusion

In modernity, the philosopher Hans Jonas states, the ethical condition of humanity underwent a radical change. For the entire history of our species, up until recently, we could take the natural world for granted. No matter what we did to each other, earth would endure. We could burn our enemy's fields to the ground, but there would be new fields to till. Our habitats might turn to desert, but we could move on to greener pastures.

But that is no longer the case. According to Jonas, writing in 1984, industrialization and the intensive burning of fossil fuels are changing the climate, and with the proliferation of nuclear weapons we have the ability to destroy our ecosystem altogether. His fear is that our inherited moral traditions are not up to these challenges that modern science and technology pose.[1]

German philosopher Jürgen Habermas, who fears for "the future of human nature," echoes Jonas's worries.[2] Whereas Jonas focuses on our impact on the natural world, Habermas concentrates on our impact on ourselves—our increasing technological ability to alter our own nature. Kant, Habermas tells us, took nature, inclusive of our own physiological nature, as a "kingdom of necessity." But for us, it is increasingly a "kingdom of contingency." We are, he contends, on the brink of an "auto-transformation of the species."[3] Our knowledge of the makeup of the human genome, coupled with the technology to manipulate it for therapeutic or enhancement purposes, makes us cocreators of future humanity in ways beyond the imagination of traditional morality and theology. Human nature at the biological level can be reengineered. And precisely as the technological possibilities opened by such advances as preimplantation genetic diagnosis, stem cells, cloning, and gene therapy become available, our moral frameworks for how to evaluate them become ever more thin and tenuous.

Consider enhancement. Athletes are regularly accused of cheating through the illicit use of anabolic steroids to enhance muscle mass. These drugs, dangerous in the long run, confer an "unfair" advantage in the short run. This has set off an arms race in some sports, a culture of clandestine steroid use, which complicates the judgment of cheating. If everyone is doing it, albeit illegally, then deviance is "defined down." Once such a culture is in place, it weakens the traditional principles of moral disapproval. If everyone can do it, how is it unfair? Those who *don't* cheat look like chumps. The other principle one might employ—that it's bad for your health and ultimately self-destructive—also looks weak. It is open to the liberal criticism of paternalism. Who are you to tell me how to live? If I want to smoke, ride my motorcycle without a helmet, use drugs, and so forth, and am only hurting myself, what has it to do with you? Thus, concerns for fairness and the welfare of persons are robbed of their ethical bite. What is left in the case of athletes is the baseline argument that such enhancement, totally at odds with the hard training, discipline, and achievement that form the essence of athletics, violates the very meaning of sports. But that, too, is open to endless disagreement. How to assert ethical control over our technology, in the absence of a full-orbed public ethic, is a formidable contemporary challenge.

The use of an exogenous agent like steroids may not present a moral challenge. But what happens when the enhancement is endogenous? What if, through gene therapy, we can change ourselves to become stronger, faster, and more vigorous? What if we can have better eyesight or live longer? Is designing a more beautiful baby analogous to the enhancement of external beauty later in life through plastic surgery? When does enhancement cross the line between the cosmetic and the constitutive? Is there such a line?

Following the secular and liberal principle of autonomy, one might grant wide latitude to individuals to enhance themselves while ruling off-limits those enhancements that are heritable or, more radically, introduced into embryos. Such interventions, one might say, delimit the autonomy and free choice of the person who will eventuate from them. Yet (someone might object) do such enhancements really differ in principle from what responsible parents already do, as when an expectant mother refrains from alcohol consumption or risky activities like skiing? Why should parents not want to give their child the best life chances? If there might someday be an intrauterine fix for intelligence, appearance, longevity, and heritable diseases, why not take advantage of it?

As in the case of steroids, one reflexive answer is that it is unfair. The wealthy will get to design their babies; the poor will be stuck in the biological dark ages. Yet would a more just arrangement alleviate the core problem? Liberal principles of autonomy or justice-as-fairness do not begin to address the profound anxieties aroused by what Habermas calls the auto-transformation of the species. Nor is it clear, in a semisecular society like ours, where the moral resources lie to address those anxieties.

Certainly, our religious traditions have much to say about the dignity of persons, but how can we articulate those teachings in the public sphere in a way that will not sidetrack but instead contribute to the democratic conversation? Those who argue that religious teaching should play no role at all do damage to the moral convictions of countless citizens. Yet those citizens must also acknowledge that the state is not a church, and that its policies require a justification that is, in principle, intelligible to all whether or not they agree with it.

Appeals to revelation, for example, fall into the category of justifications not intelligible to all. The concepts of natural law or natural theology are a different matter—if a compelling case can be made for them. Thus, many opponents of abortion base their argument not on verses of scripture or Catholic teaching but rather on natural law claims about the relation of personhood to biological nature, on the continuity of embryonic with mature human life. It remains the case, however, that the concept of natural law is itself controversial, and appraisals based on it often conflict with liberal ones. There is no court of philosophical opinion to adjudicate among the different visions of moral judgment in play in the democratic conversation.

Since antiquity, as I have noted, thinkers have sought to delineate the special dignity of human beings, whether because of their godlike rationality, in the Greek tradition, or godlike role in the Jewish one. Human persons have been thought to occupy a higher rank than animals in the chain of created beings. In the Jewish a system of law, even when capital punishment is countenanced, the taking of a human life is never a casual thing, and *halakha* greatly limits the application of the death penalty. Moreover, it surrounds the human person with protections not just in criminal law but in civil and religious law as well. In the presence of a dying person, one must beware of making movements or noises that might unduly hasten the person's demise. A religious awe, not reducible to rules or principles, envelops moments of birth and death.

Since Kant, thinkers have tried to give a postreligious grounding to this conception of human dignity—without invoking the sense of awe, the sense that a human being bears the image of God. According to Kateb in *Human Dignity*, a contemporary brief for the secularist outlook,

> It would be flattering to think ... that only human beings are in the image or likeness of the divinity and that therefore we have the dignity of kinship with some entity immeasurably greater than us but nevertheless not

utterly removed from us in its nature. . . . But we should try to do without such props; they can always give way to enlightenment.

Besides, as Kateb mentions elsewhere in the same work, given how much mischief religion has caused through the centuries, God has much blood on his hands. "Secularism relieves us of his burden."[4]

From a Jewish point of view, Kateb misstates the religious case for human dignity. Humanity does not gain its dignity by virtue of kinship with something immeasurably greater. The reason we matter is not only that God ultimately matters. We matter for who we are as persons in a world understood as replete with intrinsic value. We matter because we have the potential to advance the good that already resides, from the start, in the manifold of nature. The image of God connotes a likeness based on free, creative action. Our dignity is found in our activity and—even before we are able to act—potential for full personhood. Persons in their moral, epistemic, and creative capacities help the hidden goodness, truth, and significance of life to emerge. We have the dignity of doers, of persons who come to see their peculiarity and calling in a world otherwise composed of things.

Whether the affirmation of our freedom, creativity, and agency, when severed from religious awe, can guide us through the moral perplexities of the auto-transformation of the species is an open question. I am not inclined to believe with Fyodor Mikhaylovich Dostoyevsky and his pessimistic followers that when God is dead, all is permitted. But neither do I believe, with Kateb, that we should be relieved of "his burden." Part of what it means to be made in the image of God is that we are most emphatically *not* God. We are higher than the beasts and lower than the angels. Notwithstanding our unlimited horizon of creativity and self-transcendence, we too come from the dust. We are closer to the chimpanzee (and the worm) than Kateb wants to see.

The ambivalence of the Jewish tradition toward human nature is an attitude well worth cultivating. We are holy—and capable of unimaginable evil. Judaism reminds us of both. We have the creativity and freedom to remake the world, and now, increasingly, to remake ourselves. Our own survival might well depend on cultivating anew a sense of limits. Adam and Eve were expelled from the Garden of Eden for transgressing a limit. Limits there will always be, many imposed by human nature. Our dignity inheres in knowing when and how to master them, and when and how to accept them with respect.

Notes

Introduction

1. See Jonathan Marks, *What It Means to Be 98% Chimpanzee: Apes, People, and Their Genes* (Berkeley: University of California Press, 2002).

2. Paul Applebaum, "Blame It on My Genes," in *Neurosciences and Free Will*, ed. Robert Pollack (New York: Columbia University Press, 2009), 28–39, http://www.google.com/url?sa=t&rct=j&q=&esrc=s&source=web &cd=1&ved=0CCsQFjAA&url=http%3A%2F%2Fwww.columbia.edu% 2Fcu%2Fcssr%2Febook%2FFreeWill_eBook.pdf&ei=1D84U _bHqPCoQGmuIAQ&usg=AFQjCNGHodoOd-2q6P57MQYaX8yi XkxeEA&bvm=bv.63808443,d.dmQ (accessed May 30, 2014).

3. The scientist quoted is Cynthia Kenyon. See http://www.guardian .co.uk/science/2013/mar/17/cynthia-kenyon-rational-heroes-interview (accessed May 30, 2014). For a strong claim that scientific language that ascribes personal properties to brains (rather than whole human beings) is categorically mistaken and attempted rebuttals, see Maxwell Bennett, Daniel Dennett, Peter Hacker, and John R. Searle, *Neuroscience & Philosophy: Brain, Mind, & Language* (New York: Columbia University Press, 2007).

4. Steven Pinker, *The Blank Slate: The Modern Denial of Human Nature* (New York: Penguin Books, 2002), 55; emphasis added.

5. Donald E. Brown, "Human Universals," *Daedalus* 133, no. 4 (Fall 2004): 47–54.

6. Peter Singer, *Unsanctifying Human Life*, ed. Helga Kühse (Malden, MA: Blackwell Publishing, 2002).

7. For a fascinating attempt to give a scientific account of the soul, see Lenn E. Goodman and B. Gregory Caramenico, *Coming to Mind: The Soul and Its Body* (Chicago: University of Chicago Press, 2013).

8. The Chinese philosopher Mencius (fourth century BCE) elegantly

captures the polarity between concepts of human nature and human personhood in the following: "The way that the mouth is disposed towards tastes, the eye towards colours, the nose towards odours, the limbs towards ease is human nature (*hsing*). Yet there is *ming* (the moral law). So the refined person does not choose to say 'human nature.' The way that benevolence pertains to fathers and sons, duty to prince and subject, propriety to guest and host, wisdom to the virtuous and wise, and the sage to the ways of heaven is *ming* (divine decree). Yet there is *hsing* (human nature). So the refined person does not choose to say '*ming*.'" Mencius juxtaposes the basal, natural condition of the human with its higher realizations in morally framed personhood. These are mutually dependent, complementary conditions. Ning Chen, "The Concept of Fate in Mencius," *Philosophy East and West* 47 (1997): 496; quoted in Lenn E. Goodman, *Jewish and Islamic Philosophy: Cross-Pollinations in the Classical Age* (New Brunswick, NJ: Rutgers University Press, 1999), 81–82.

9. Robert B. Louden, *Kant's Human Being: Essays on His Theory of Human Nature* (New York: Oxford University Press, 2011), xviii.

10. For two classics, see Samuel Belkin, *In His Image: The Jewish Philosophy of Man as Expressed in Rabbinic Tradition* (New York: Abelard-Schuman, 1960); Abraham Joshua Heschel, *Who Is Man?* (Stanford, CA: Stanford University Press, 1965). For other useful works, see Louis Jacobs, *Religion and the Individual: A Jewish Perspective* (Cambridge: Cambridge University Press, 1992); Martin Buber, "What Is Man?" in *Between Man and Man* (New York: Macmillan, 1965). (Buber's book is not explicitly Jewish but nevertheless reflects his dialogic-Judaic perspective.) For a compendium of relevant sources, see Ephraim E. Urbach, *The Sages*, trans. Israel Abrahams (Cambridge, MA: Harvard University Press, 1979), 214–55.

11. Wilfred Sellars, "Philosophy and the Scientific Image of Man," in *Science, Perception, and Reality* (Atascadero, CA: Ridgeview Publishing Co., 1991), 1–40.

12. In *Jewish Faith and Modern Science* (Lanham, MD: Rowman and Littlefield, 2008), Norbert Samuelson argues that modern Jewish philosophy's neglect of science has ensured its irrelevance as a valid intellectual option. That seems an overstatement to me.

13. Richard Rorty, *Philosophy and Social Hope* (London: Penguin Books, 1999), 168.

14. See Ludwig Wittgenstein, *Philosophical Investigations*, trans. G.E.M. Anscombe (New York: Macmillan, 1968), paragraphs 23, 241.

15. John Cottingham, *The Spiritual Dimension: Religion, Philosophy, and Human Value* (Cambridge: Cambridge University Press, 2005), 5.

16. I didn't always disagree. My first book took this very stance. See Alan Mittleman, *Between Kant and Kabbalah: An Introduction to Isaac Breuer's Philosophy of Judaism* (Albany: State University of New York Press, 1990).

17. Michael Oakeshott, *Rationalism in Politics and Other Essays* (Indianapolis: Liberty Fund, 1991), 488.

CHAPTER 1: PERSONS IN A WORLD OF THINGS

1. Martin Buber, *Between Man and Man* (New York: Macmillan, 1965), 126.

2. Quoted in ibid., 126.

3. Ibid., 126.

4. Ibid., 132.

5. Martin Buber, *P'nei Adam* (Jerusalem: Mossad Bialik, 1962), 12.

6. Abraham Joshua Heschel, *Who Is Man?* (Stanford, CA: Stanford University Press, 1965), 22, 28, 111.

7. Francis Crick, *The Astonishing Hypothesis: The Scientific Search for the Soul* (New York: Scribner, 1994), 3.

8. Quoted in Raymond Tallis, *Aping Mankind: Neuromania, Darwinitis, and the Misrepresentation of Humanity* (Durham, UK: Acumen Publishing, 2011), 120.

9. Wilfred Sellars, *Science, Perception, and Reality* (Atascadero, CA: Ridgeview Publishing Co., 1991), 16.

10. By complete image, Sellars means that while all the streams of science make their contributions, physics ultimately settles matters because all the other scientific perspectives are in principle answerable to it. Ibid., 20.

11. Ibid., 26.

12. Ibid., 39.

13. Ibid., 40.

14. Thomas Nagel, *The Last Word* (New York: Oxford University Press, 1997), 19.

15. Ibid., 21. On the idea of debunking explanations and the perils of using them, see Guy Kahane, "Evolutionary Debunking Arguments," *NOUS* 45, no. 1 (2011): 103–25.

16. Immanuel Kant, *Critique of Practical Reason*, trans. Lewis White Beck (Upper Saddle River, NJ: Prentice Hall, 1993), 86.

17. Tallis, *Aping Mankind*, 10.

18. Thomas Nagel, *The View from Nowhere* (Oxford: Oxford University Press, 1986), 9.

19. Ibid., 9, quoted in Alan Thomas, *Thomas Nagel* (Durham, UK: Acumen Publishing, 2009), 2.

20. This last example is from John Dupré, criticizing Patricia Churchland, in John Dupré, *The Disorder of Things: Metaphysical Foundations of the Disunity of Science* (Cambridge, MA: Harvard University Press, 1995), 158.

21. For the Kantian account treated here, see Immanuel Kant, *Groundwork of the Metaphysic of Morals*, trans. H. J. Paton (New York: Harper Torchbooks, 1956). To explore Kant's larger framing of human nature, particularly with respect to the categories of rational beings and persons, see Robert B. Louden, *Kant's Human Being: Essays on His Theory of Human Nature* (New York: Oxford University Press, 2011). In Kant's mature anthropological theory, human nature and personhood bleed into each other, as already indicated here in the *Groundwork*.

22. Kant, *Groundwork*, 119.

23. Ibid., 96; emphasis added.

24. Immanuel Kant, "On a Supposed Right to Lie from Altruistic Motives," http://www.mesacc.edu/~davpy35701/text/kant-sup-right-to-lie .pdf (accessed October 30, 2013).

25. Noted Kant scholar Allen Wood accepts just such a view. "For better or worse," Wood writes, "Kantian principles (rightly understood) justify attaching great importance to preserving human life, at least most of the time, but they provide no support for the idea that, as some people like to put it, 'all human life is sacred.'" His footnote to the latter phrase leads to this: "Peter Singer is no Kantian, but I think a Kantian could (or even should) agree with a lot of what he has said against the doctrine of the sacredness of human life." Allen W. Wood, *Kantian Ethics* (New York: Cambridge University Press, 2008), 87. Since Kant's criterion for personhood is rationality and since what counts for someone like Singer is the capacity of animals (and humans) to suffer, not to reason, the moral status of personhood for Singer is contingent on the ability to suffer. I don't see how Kant could accept that personhood be constituted in this way, nor do I see why Kantians should. All this suggests that the traditional biblical doctrine of the sacredness of human life may have few friends even among the modern philosophical tradition most compatible with it.

26. British analytic philosopher G.E.M. Anscombe sensed incoherence

in a project like Kant's, and urged a reconsideration of Jewish and Christian materials. See her seminal essay "Modern Moral Philosophy," reprinted in G.E.M. Anscombe, *The Collected Papers of G.E.M. Anscombe, Vol. III: Ethics, Religion, and Politics* (Minneapolis: University of Minnesota Press, 1981), 27. For a particularly enthusiastic contemporary endorsement of this approach, see Harry Frankfurt, "Reflections of My Career in Philosophy," *Proceedings and Addresses of the American Philosophical Association* 85, no. 2 (November 2011): 106.

27. Joseph B. Soloveitchik, *The Emergence of Ethical Man*, ed. Michael Berger (Hoboken, NJ: Toras HaRov Foundation, 2005). As early as the 1950s, Soloveitchik wrote of his interest in a philosophical perspective on "the doctrine of man" and "field of religious anthropology" (ibid., xii).

28. Ibid., 12.

29. Ibid., 60.

30. Soloveitchik's premise that animals learn departs from the earlier view that grounds the distinctiveness of human nature on the capacity for learning. See, for example, the work of eighteenth-century Jewish philosopher (and student of Kant) Solomon Maimon, *Givat Ha-Moreh*, ed. Nathan Rotenstreich and Samuel H. Bergman (Jerusalem: Israeli Academy of Sciences and Humanities, 1965), 1. Maimon sharply distinguishes between animals, whose nature is such that they do what they need to do to survive through innate necessity, and humans, whose nature it is to learn to do what must be done. This fits into Maimon's larger story about perfection: the more perfect a being is, the more it brings its ends from potentiality into actuality. Humans are more perfect than any animal insofar as they must learn how to actualize their ends. To the degree that *we* have learned a great deal about animal learning, Soloveitchik's view is far more appropriate than Maimon's.

31. Soloveitchik, *The Emergence of Ethical Man*, 74.

32. Ibid., 75.

33. Ibid., 78.

CHAPTER 2: PERSONS IN THE IMAGE OF GOD

1. B. Sanhedrin 105a.

2. Bernard Williams, *Truth and Truthfulness* (Princeton, NJ: Princeton University Press, 2002), 20–21.

3. Rashi (Rabbi Solomon ben Isaac) says that the Torah did not come to

give us a "*seder ha-beriah*," an order of creation, but instead to give Israel a title to the land of Israel. No doubt Rashi believed that Adam, Eve, and the others actually existed. The point is that Rashi did not think the Torah's purpose here was to narrate a standard history but rather to establish the context for Israel's covenantal relationship with God and its claim to the land of Israel.

4. The Talmud mordantly acknowledges that people in fact do all these bad things, inviting us to imagine how much worse off we would be if we had *not* been created equal.

5. See, for example, Stuart Kauffman, *Reinventing the Sacred: A New View of Science, Reason, and Religion* (New York: Basic Books, 2008); Holmes Ralston III, *Three Big Bangs: Matter-Energy, Life, Mind* (New York: Columbia University Press, 2010), 121–24. See also Terrence W. Deacon, *Incomplete Nature: How Mind Emerged from Matter* (New York: W. W. Norton, 2012), especially 107–81. For a more robustly theistic (and Judaic) argument, see Lenn E. Goodman, *Creation and Evolution* (New York: Routledge, 2010), 138–44.

6. In the view of the medieval Jewish thinker Naḥmanides (1194–1270), a formless matter, drawn out of nothingness, contained all possible actualities. Subsequent creation consisted of this pure potentiality. See Naḥmanides on Genesis 1:1. Thanks to such "scientific" interpretations, which reflected the absorption of ancient Hellenistic philosophical thought about nature, modern religious Jews were not monolithically hostile to evolutionary theory. Like many nineteenth- and twentieth-century Christians, they thought that "theistic evolution" was the best explanation for the cosmos and the natural history of the earth. Evolutionary theory itself does not necessarily warrant the current emphasis among atheistic debunkers on its subversive implications. For a discussion, see Goodman, *Creation and Evolution*.

7. Unless otherwise noted, all biblical translations are from *Tanakh: The Holy Scriptures* (Philadelphia: Jewish Publication Society, 1988).

8. Ralston (*Three Big Bangs*, 114) provides a secular analogue to the Psalmist's rumination on human value in the teeth of insignificance: "Earth is a lonely planet, lost out there in the stars; humans are latecomers on Earth, arriving in the last few seconds of geological and astronomical time. We are cosmic dwarfs, trivial on the universal scale. Copernicus dealt a cosmological blow: humans do not live at the center of the universe. Darwin struck an evolutionary blow: humans are not divine but animals. [James D.] Watson and Crick struck a molecular-biology blow: humans are nothing

but electronic molecules in motion on atomic scales. [Sigmund] Freud struck a psychological blow, the most humiliating of all: we persons are not masters of our own minds. But with a gestalt switch, one can read the same natural history to find cosmic genius in humans."

9. Thus *The Fathers according to Rabbi Nathan* (*Avot de-Rabbi Natan*), an ancient rabbinic commentary on Mishnah Avot, claims that human beings are ultimately superior to all the existents created before them because only humans can understand the whole. Judah Goldin, trans., *The Fathers according to Rabbi Nathan*, Yale Judaica Series (New Haven, CT: Yale University Press, 1955), 10:152.

10. W. Randall Garr, *In His Own Image and Likeness: Humanity, Divinity, and Monotheism* (Leiden: Brill, 2003), 125. By contrast, a modern Jewish exegete, Umberto Cassuto, believes that by the time the biblical author used tzelem and d'mut, these terms had already lost their connotation of visibility and physicality. Cassuto seems somewhat apologetic here. Umberto Cassuto, *From Adam to Noah: A Commentary on Genesis I–V* [in Hebrew] (Jerusalem: Magnes, 1953), 34.

11. Garr, *In His Own Image and Likeness*, 140.

12. Andreas Schüle, "Made in the 'Image of God': The Concepts of Divine Images in Gen. 1–3," *Zeitschrift für die alttestamentliche Wissenschaft* 117, no. 1 (July 2005): 10.

13. For Maimonides, ascribing a body and physicality to God draws God into the world of things; it makes the Creator a creature. A more profound and sinful error is inconceivable. To have a body is to be limited, place bound, and partite. But Maimonides's view, congenial to all subsequent religious rationalists, met with opposition in his own lifetime. His sharpest legal critic, Rabbi Abraham ben David of Posquieres, in his glosses to Maimonides's *Mishneh Torah* writes, "Why does he [Maimonides] call one a heretic [who believes that God has a body and an image]? Persons greater and better than he have believed this on the basis of the Bible and even more so on the basis of the aggadah." See *Hasagat ha-Ravad* on H. *Teshuva* 3:7. The appropriateness of anthropomorphism among nonphilosophical Jews is an enduring theme. For a thorough treatment, see Yair Lorberbaum, *The Image of God: Halakhah and Aggadah* [in Hebrew] (Jerusalem: Schocken Publishing, 2004). (Lorberbaum's work is controversial, however. For a critique, see Joseph Isaac Lifshitz, "Defining Divinity Down," *Azure* 20 [2005] 129–33.) For a strong defense and explication of ancient and medieval rabbinic anthropomorphism, see Alon Goshen-Gottstein, "The Body as Image

of God in Rabbinic Literature," *Harvard Theological Review* 87, no. 2 (April 1994): 171–95. As Goshen-Gottstein (ibid., 173) writes, "If God has a body, then obviously the creation of man in God's image refers to man's physical form. There is absolutely no objection in all of rabbinic literature to such an interpretation." For another contemporary defense of divine anthropomorphism, see Benjamin D. Sommer, *The Bodies of God and the World of Ancient Israel* (New York: Cambridge University Press, 2009).

14. Garr, *In His Own Image and Likeness*, 127. Taking a different view, Schüle ("Made in the 'Image of God,'" 19) sees the creation of the human in Genesis 2 as going beyond and even criticizing the "passive" definition of persons in Genesis 1 as made in the image of God.

15. Goshen-Gottstein, "The Body as the Image of God," 195.

16. Ibid., 192.

17. Quoted in ibid., 175. Cf. Shabbat 50b and Rashi ad loc.

18. In Leon Kass's view, humans do not yet merit being called "good" because they are radically unfinished. Insofar as humans make themselves through their moral choices, they have the possibility to become good. The lacuna, for Kass, is meant to indicate this existential reality and, accordingly, a suspension of divine judgment. Leon R. Kass, *The Beginning of Wisdom: Reading Genesis* (New York: Free Press, 2003), 39.

19. There are many interpretations of this "us." Genesis Rabba (8:3) itself presents God as taking counsel with heaven and earth—that is, with all created things; with a council of advisers whom He trusts; with His own heart; and with a delegated agent who merely does His bidding. The late medieval exegete Isaac Abravanel helpfully systematized subsequent views into two basic approaches. In the first, the earth and the power of nature contribute the vital organic dimensions of the human being, and God provides the spiritual dimension. The term *us* therefore refers to God and nature as partners in humanity's birth. Humanity is a divine/natural hybrid; "our image and likeness" expresses this hybridity. Abravanel notes that R. David Kimḥi, Naḥmanides, and Gersonides all followed this path. The second approach favors the angels—the heavenly retinue—as the referent, with God, of *us*. In this view, humanity is distinguished not by its hybridity but instead by its distinctive rationality. God and the earth together created all the other creatures, but humanity's creation is radically different in kind. For the medievals, the angels are understood in Aristotelian terms as "separate intelligences," essentially transcendent ideas similar to Platonic forms. See *Perush Abravanel 'al ha-Torah*, Genesis 1:26 ad loc.

20. The midrash tries to establish that God, knowing that human beings would be good for Him, can ignore the angels' counsel. The letters that form Adam—*aleph, daled, mem*—when rearranged, form the word very (*m'od—mem, aleph, daled*). Thus, the statement at the conclusion of creation—"And God saw all that He had made and found it *very* good" (Gen. 1:31)—is taken by the midrash to refer to the creation of humanity.

21. "Till you grow old, I will still be the same; When you turn gray, it is I who will carry; I was the Maker, and I will be the Bearer; And I will carry you and rescue [you]" (Isaiah 46:4). The text is found at B. Sanhedrin 38b.

22. The prayer alludes, through careful choice of language, to both the creation story—the *tohu va-vohu* (unformed and void) of Genesis 1:2—and the repeated invocation in Ecclesiastes of the vanity or futility (hevel) of all things. Alone among biblical books, Ecclesiastes strikes a strongly pessimistic note. This prayer, however, does not follow Ecclesiastes in that way. Immediately after the quoted passage, it qualifies and indeed repudiates its pessimism by invoking God's covenant with Israel, recalling the deeds of Abraham, and calling the Jews to recognize their obligation to praise God and live godly lives.

23. Here God's own attributes are the implicit referents of us.

24. For a useful book that presents a concise, philosophically lucid analysis of Plato's writings and much else, see Stewart Goetz and Charles Taliaferro, *A Brief History of the Soul* (Malden, MA: Wiley-Blackwell, 2011), 15.

25. The tendency among modern interpreters has been to locate the rabbinic view of the yetzer ha-ra within the ancient Hellenistic "discourse of self-control and self-fashioning." The best contemporary scholar of the subject, however, claims that the yetzer ha-ra should be understood as a demonic presence: a separate animallike entity that tries to invade us and cause us to err. Its proper context, in other words, is not Hellenistic moral psychology but rather Jewish and Christian demonology. See Ishay Rosen-Zvi, *Demonic Desires: Yetzer Hara and the Problem of Evil in Late Antiquity* (Philadelphia: University of Pennsylvania Press, 2011), 6. For a compilation of sources, see Ephraim E. Urbach, *The Sages*, trans. Israel Abrahams (Cambridge, MA: Harvard University Press, 1979), 471–83.

26. On the basis of t'shuka's occurrence in the biblical text, Genesis Rabba 20:7 enumerates several instances of this word, meaning strong desire verging on eros: the desire of a woman for her husband, the desire of the evil inclination for Cain and his descendants, the desire of rain for the earth,

and the desire of God for Israel. For an exemplary instance of t'shuka in the Bible, see Song of Songs 7:11.

27. The midrash asks why "sin," a feminine noun, takes a masculine verb; it answers that sin begins to work in a weak, "feminine" way and becomes powerful, in a masculine way, as it develops.

28. The midrash takes the verb in Gen. 1:26, *va-yirdu*, "he shall rule," as if its root were *y-r-d* (they will descend) rather than *r-d-h*. On the substance of this midrash, compare Sanhedrin 38b: "Rami b. Hama said: 'A wild beast has no dominion over man unless he appears to it as a brute, for it is written, "Men are overruled when they appear as beasts"'" (Ps. 49:13). In Genesis Rabba 22:12, the animals surround Cain after he has killed Abel. Previously in awe of him, they lost their fear when he became a murderer; the animals then sought to avenge his brother. God's promise of protection to Cain here signifies protection against the animals who—for reasons of justice, as they understand it—want to kill him.

29. Joseph Albo, *Sefer Ha-Ikkarim: The Book of Principles*, trans. Isaac Husik (Philadelphia: Jewish Publication Society, 1946), 3:128–37.

30. Ibid., 3:129, 130.

31. Ibid., 3:133. Thus, on Albo's view, the somewhat-obscure biblical word uplift means "lifted above the animals." Cassuto (*From Adam to Noah*), following traditional exegetes, more plausibly suggests that uplift refers to the lifting up of Cain's "fallen" face.

32. Albo, *Sefer Ha-Ikkarim*, 3:134. When I was in college in the early 1970s, I heard the late Krister Stendahl argue that Cain's question, "Am I my brother's keeper?" was not disingenuous but sincere. Many years later, when we had become friends, Stendahl confirmed his reading of the verse as ascribing a certain naïveté to Cain. His point was that the word keeper (*shomer*) is often used with regard to animals, and Cain did not think that his relationship to Abel, a human being, was like that of a human to an animal. Albo makes precisely the opposite point, but he also sees Cain as, in a sense, naive.

33. Compare the polemic of the anthropologist Jonathan Marks against the "human rights" movement on behalf of the great apes: "A concern for animal welfare must come out of a concern for *human* welfare. It must emerge from a concern for human rights, not supplant it. For once we begin to devalue human lives, we lose a standard by which to value any other kind of lives. And it just doesn't work the other way around." Jonathan Marks, *What It Means to Be 98% Chimpanzee: Apes, People, and Their Genes* (Berke-

ley: University of California Press, 2002), 195. Directly opposed to this are animal rights philosophers like Martha Nussbaum who advocate not simply compassion but also justice for animals on the basis of their capacities for flourishing in their own ways. Martha C. Nussbaum, *Frontiers of Justice: Disability, Nationality, Species Membership* (Cambridge, MA: Harvard University Press, 2006), 325–407.

34. Genesis Rabba 18:6, *Avot de Rabbi Natan*, 10.

35. I owe these insights to Barnard College professor Beth Berkowitz, who shared her as yet unpublished paper on animals in rabbinic law with me. See Beth Berkowitz, "Animal," in *Late Ancient Knowing: New Intellectual History*, ed. Catherine M. Chin and Moulie Vidas (Berkeley: University of California Press, forthcoming).

36. Maimonides observes that "the sensation which is in one species [is not] the same sensation which is in another species. Rather, every single species having a soul possesses a unique soul, different from the soul of another [species]." Like human beings, plants and animals have nutritive dimensions to their souls, but those souls perform their functions in ways specific to the beings that have them. Maimonides, "Eight Chapters," in *Ethical Writings of Maimonides*, ed. Raymond L. Weiss and Charles Butterworth (Mineola, NY: Dover Publications, 1983), 62.

37. Hume, owing to his empiricism and naturalism, has become a kind of heroic ancestor for neurophilosophers. See, for example, Patricia S. Churchland, *Braintrust: What Neuroscience Tells Us about Morality* (Princeton, NJ: Princeton University Press, 2011), 5–6. The neuroscientist Antonio Damasio, an expert on the neuroscience of emotion, has rediscovered Spinoza; see his *Looking for Spinoza: Joy, Sorrow, and the Feeling Brain* (New York: Harcourt, 2003). For a typical denunciation of Descartes ("Descartes and Other Disasters"), see John R. Searle, *Mind: A Brief Introduction* (New York: Oxford University Press, 2004), 8 ff. Descartes, though, is not without defenders. See Daniel N. Robinson, *Consciousness and Mental Life* (New York: Columbia University Press, 2008), 51–81.

38. On the essentially moral constitution of the concept of the self, see Charles Taylor, *Sources of the Self: The Making of the Modern Identity* (Cambridge, MA: Harvard University Press, 1989), 25–52.

39. The trope of a god breathing life into human beings is common in ancient Egypt, Mesopotamia, and Canaan. For an overview of the scholarly literatures and primary sources, see Admiel Kosman, "Breath, Kiss, and Speech as the Source of the Animation of Life: Ancient Foundations of

Rabbinic Homilies on the Giving of the Torah as the Kiss of God," in *Self, Soul, and Body in Religious Experience*, ed. Albert I. Baumgarten, Jan Assmann, and Gedaliahu A. G. Stroumsa (Leiden: Brill, 1998), 99–102.

40. Schüle has shown that in ancient Babylonian and Assyrian ceremonies for sanctifying the images (statues) of gods, the mouth of the statue was symbolically opened; from that point on, the god/image was thought to breathe and therefore be alive. The next phase was to bring the image to a garden located by a river. After sojourning there, the god is taken to his temple for permanent habitation. From this perspective, God's breathing into man and vitalizing him (as well as placing him in a garden) is reminiscent of ancient Near Eastern ritual practices. Schüle, "Made in the 'Image of God,'" 12.

41. Death also forms a single community: when, in the time of Noah, God judges all on earth to be irredeemably wicked, all were destroyed "in whose nostrils was the merest breath of life [*nishmat ruah hayim*]" (Gen. 7:22).

42. For background, see Gershom Scholem, *Major Trends in Jewish Mysticism* (New York: Schocken, 1995), 240. For the development of the concept of the soul in kabbalah, see Isaiah Tishbi, ed., *The Wisdom of the Zohar: An Anthology of Texts* (Oxford: Littman Library of Jewish Civilization, 1989), 2:677 ff.

43. Joel B. Green, "Soul," in *New Interpreter's Dictionary of the Bible*, ed. Katharine Doob Sakenfeld (Nashville, TN: Abingdon Press, 2009), 5:359. See also Ps. 104:1. For a full treatment of the many senses of nefesh in the Hebrew Bible, see Joel B. Green, *Body, Soul, and Human Life: The Nature of Humanity in the Bible* (Grand Rapids, MI: Baker Academic, 2008), 54. Green points out that the exact meaning of terms like nefesh and basar, or *psyche* and *soma* in Greek philosophy and the New Testament, depends heavily on the context. Flat translations like soul and body are laden with centuries of semantic baggage, and are singularly unhelpful terms.

44. See also Ps. 33:18–19. "Truly the eye of the LORD is on those who fear Him, who wait for his faithful care to save them [*nafsham*] from death, to sustain them in famine. We [*nafsheynu*] set our hope on the LORD." The words translated as "them" and "we" are instances of nefesh, which here functions as a term for person. If it had the sense of an immortal entity, the notion of sustaining it through famine would be absurd.

45. This dualism should not be overdrawn. According to Kosman ("Breath, Kiss, and Speech," 106), rabbinic sources from the Land of Israel

did not distinguish between the terms breathing (*neshima*) and soul (ne-shama). The sources also see God as responsible for each breath that one takes. Thus, in at least some cases, the distinction between a person and their soul is analogous to that between a person and their breath.

46. Cf. Brevard S. Childs, *Old Testament Theology in a Canonical Context* (Philadelphia: Fortress Press, 1985), 199. For a comprehensive overview, see Reuven Kimelman, "The Rabbinic Theology of the Physical: Blessings, Body and Soul, Resurrection, and Covenant and Election," in *The Late Roman-Rabbinic Period*, ed. Steven T. Katz (New York: Cambridge University Press, 2006). For a study of the soul/body relationship in a key rabbinic source for this topic, see Burton L. Visotzky, *Golden Bells and Pomegranates: Studies in Midrash Leviticus Rabbah* (Tübingen: Mohr Siebeck, 2003), 90–98.

47. The prayer first appears in the gemara, B. Berakhot 60b. See also B. Shabbat 152b, where the soul is compared to the garments of a king. The king gives his garments to his courtiers. The wise courtiers take care of them, while the foolish ones work in them and dirty them. When the king comes to retrieve his garments, he is pleased with the careful servants and angry with the irresponsible ones. Thus, we are enjoined to care for our pure souls and return them to God in a state akin to the one in which they were given.

48. Elie Munk, *The World of Prayer* (New York: Feldheim Publishers, n.d.), 1:21–22. For historical context, see Ismar Elbogen, *Jewish Liturgy: A Comprehensive History*, trans. Raymond P. Scheindlin (Philadelphia: Jewish Publication Society, 1993), 78.

49. For an accessible yet profound study of the belief in resurrection in biblical Israel, and then in Judaism and Christianity, see Kevin J. Madigan and Jon D. Levenson, *Resurrection: The Power of God for Christians and Jews* (New Haven, CT: Yale University Press, 2008). On the "psycho-physical" holism of the biblical view of the nefesh, see ibid., 109.

50. Visotzky (*Golden Bells and Pomegranates*, 93) points out that this parable, which also appears in Leviticus Rabba and Mekilta de-Rabbi Ishmael, has Greco-Roman antecedents and Christian parallels. Unlike the pagan and Christian deployments, however, the rabbinic versions do not blame the body as the source of impurity and corruption. If anything, they blame the soul more than the body. As an ethereal being, it should know better, as it were. For a midrash that elaborates on the parallels between soul and God, see ibid., 97–98.

51. The chief Aristotelian, of course, is Maimonides. For his treatments

of the soul, see especially the first chapter of Maimonides, "Eight Chapters," 61–64.

52. Jonathan Barnes, *Aristotle: A Very Short Introduction* (Oxford: Oxford University Press, 2000), 107.

53. Saadya Gaon, *The Book of Doctrines and Beliefs*, in *Three Jewish Philosophers*, ed. Hans Lewy, Alexander Altmann, and Isaak Heinemann (New York: Atheneum, 1969), 142. For Aristotle's treatment, see *On the Soul*, book 2, section 1.

54. A distant descendant of Aristotle's approach is contemporary philosopher John Searle's view that thought is to the brain what digestion is to the stomach—that is, a demystified natural functioning of an organ.

55. Saadya, *Book of Doctrines and Beliefs*, 143.

56. Ibid., 145.

57. Ibid., 149.

58. Ibid., 150.

59. Ibid., 151. In the eyes of halakha, bodily substances are impure only after they have left the body. Whether Saadya is claiming that this legal categorization is in some sense arbitrary, a product of divine command unrelated to the substances themselves, is unclear.

60. For a discussion of this highly sensitive point, see Alan Mittleman, *A Short History of Jewish Ethics* (Oxford: Wiley-Blackwell, 2012), 61–69. For Albo's discussion, see Albo, *Sefer Ha-Ikkarim*, 4:273–88.

61. Ibid., 3:23–34.

62. Ibid., 4:284–85.

63. This can readily be seen in another major medieval philosopher, Baḥya ben Joseph ibn Pakuda. In the *Duties of the Heart*, we are enjoined to meditate on the wisdom of God's creation, which we might do by considering the ensouled body of humans. The end here is moral, but also religious in a broad sense: awe, wonder, and inward turning to conform to God's ways in all respects. See Baḥya ben Joseph ibn Pakuda, *The Book of Direction to the Duties of the Heart*, trans. Menahem Mansoor (Oxford: Littman Library of Jewish Civilization, 2004), 160 ff.

64. Taylor, *Sources of the Self*, 34.

65. Richard Moran, *Authority and Estrangement: An Essay on Self-Knowledge* (Princeton, NJ: Princeton University Press, 2001), 32.

66. For a leading biologist's perspective on the relation between genetic and cultural evolution, see Edward O. Wilson, *On Human Nature* (Cambridge, MA: Harvard University Press, 1978), 79–80. For an overview of the

relations between biology and culture, see Melvin Konner, *The Tangled Wing: Biological Constraints on the Human Spirit* (New York: Henry Holt and Co., 2002).

67. Taylor, *Sources of the Self*, 35.

68. Ibid., 36.

69. Taylor (ibid., 49) points out that the kinds of question typically asked by modern philosophers of mind about consciousness, self-consciousness, identity over time, and so on, bleach out the moral, normative dimensions of selfhood. The public dimension of relationality, the web of interlocution in which normative questions of identity and value are raised, is suppressed in favor of an allegedly neutral analysis of the self. By way of contrast with this modernist conception of selfhood, an emphasis on the normative as opposed to the epistemological suits the Jewish sources well, as their concept of selfhood is relational rather than atomistic. Significantly, modernist Jewish thinkers who write on selfhood, including Buber and Emmanuel Levinas, tend strongly to resist the kind of analysis promulgated by epistemology.

70. As Wilson (*On Human Nature*, 137) observes, "The most distinctive feature of the sexual bond, one of overriding significance for human social organization, is that it transcends sexual activity."

71. Quoted in Naftali Rothenberg, *Wisdom of Love: Man, Woman, and God in Jewish Canonical Literature* (Boston: Academic Studies Press, 2009), 23. For parallels of the primordial androgyne motif, see B. Berachot 61a; Leviticus Rabba 14:1; Midrash on Psalms 139.

72. Cf. Genesis Rabba 17:2; Sotah 17a; Niddah 31a; Rashi ad loc.

73. For a sociobiological approach to homosexuality, see Wilson, *On Human Nature*, 142–47.

74. Ibid., 116.

75. The midrash (Tanḥuma, Bereshit 11) offers a profoundly different reading: it exculpates Lamech. In this reworking of the story, Lamech is blind and is being led out to hunt by his young son. The son tells him of a beast with a horn in the distance. Lamech shoots and kills the creature. On closer inspection, however, the son tells him that it is actually a man with a horn on his forehead. Lamech realizes that it is his ancestor, Cain. (In another midrash, the protective "mark of Cain" is a horn.) In his contrition, Lamech slaps his hands together, inadvertently hitting his young son in the head and killing him. He then recites the words of Genesis 4:23, which the midrash reads as follows: "By a wound of mine [my blindness] I slew a man,

and by a blow of mine [clapping my hands] a child." Quoted in Hayim Nah-man Bialik and Yehoshua Hana Ravnitzky, *The Book of Legends (Sefer Ha-Aggadah)*, trans. William G. Braude (New York: Schocken Books, 1992), 24.

76. Konner, *Tangled Wing*, 8.

77. Alasdair MacIntyre, *Dependent, Rational Animals* (Peru, IL: Open Court Publishing Co., 1999), 1.

78. Franz Rosenzweig, *The Star of Redemption* (Madison: University of Wisconsin Press, 2005), 82.

79. Moses Maimonides, *The Guide of the Perplexed*, trans. Shlomo Pines (Chicago: University of Chicago Press, 1963), 1:22.

80. Ibid., 2:632–38.

81. Ibid., 2:635.

82. Ibid., 2:638.

83. Michael Fox's comment is apt: "The postscript in 12:13–14 reminds us that wisdom, originating in human intellect and tradition, takes second rank to piety and obedience to God's law. The words of the wise are not always comfortable, pious, and traditional as the books of Ecclesiastes and Job prove." Michael V. Fox, ed., *Ecclesiastes: The JPS Bible Commentary* (Philadelphia: Jewish Publication Society, 2004), 83.

84. Whether you can coherently conceive such a creature is another problem, however. See Todd C. Moody, "Conversations with Zombies," *Journal of Consciousness Studies* 1, no. 2 (1994): 196–200.

85. Nagel popularized the vague but provocative notion of what it is like to be something. See Thomas Nagel, "What Is It Like to Be a Bat?" *Philosophical Review* 83, no. 4 (October 1974): 435–50. For a critique of this concept when it comes to the study of consciousness, see Maxwell Bennett, Daniel Dennett, Peter Hacker, and John R. Searle, *Neuroscience and Philosophy: Brain, Mind, and Language* (New York: Columbia University Press, 2007), 40–42.

86. Damasio, *Looking for Spinoza*, 86. See also Antonio Damasio, *Self Comes to Mind* (New York: Vintage Books, 2010), 67–94.

87. Damasio, *Looking for Spinoza*, 12.

88. Quoted in John R. Searle, *The Mystery of Consciousness* (New York: New York Review of Books, 1997), 101.

89. Michael Gazzaniga, *Who's in Charge? Free Will and the Science of the Brain* (New York: Ecco Books, 2012), 102.

90. Ibid., 103.

91. For an example of this, see Paul M. Churchland, *The Engine of Reason, the Seat of the Soul* (Cambridge, MA: MIT Press, 1996), 322.

92. Deacon, *Incomplete Nature*, 175.

93. Quoted in Griff Rhys Jones, ed., *The Nation's Favourite: Twentieth Century Poems* (London: BBC Books, 1999), 100.

CHAPTER 3: ARE PERSONS FREE TO CHOOSE?

1. Some readers will be aware of the famous sixteenth-century debate between Desiderius Erasmus and Martin Luther on the freedom (or bondage) of the will. That debate turned on whether human beings can exercise reason and will to work toward salvation, or whether they are so marred by original sin, and so in need of grace, that their wills are powerless. Jewish sources, with their emphasis on the possibility of repentance, do not construct the issue in this way.

2. Francis Crick, *The Astonishing Hypothesis* (New York: Touchstone, 1994), 3.

3. Edward O. Wilson, *On Human Nature* (Cambridge, MA: Harvard University Press, 1978), 71. See also Edward O. Wilson, *Consilience: The Unity of Knowledge* (New York: Vintage Books, 1998), 130–32.

4. Philip Kitcher, *Vaulting Ambition: Sociobiology and the Quest for Human Nature* (Cambridge, MA: MIT Press, 1987), 407.

5. "Whatever you are, you can't influence the undetermined event—the whole point of quantum indeterminacy is that such quantum events are not influenced by anything." Daniel Dennett, *Freedom Evolves* (New York: Viking, 2003), 123.

6. René Descartes, *The Passions of the Soul*, part I, para. 41, http://www.earlymoderntexts.com/pdfbits/despass1.pdf (accessed June 4, 2014).

7. David Hume, *A Treatise of Human Nature* (Oxford: Clarendon Press, 1975), book 3, sections 1–3, 399–412.

8. Harry G. Frankfurt, "Freedom of the Will," in *The Importance of What We Care About* (New York: Cambridge University Press, 1998). "It is in securing the conformity of his will to his second-order volitions, then, that a person exercises freedom of the will" (ibid., 20).

9. Michael Gazzaniga, *Who's in Charge? Free Will and the Science of the Brain* (New York: Ecco Books, 2012), 119.

10. Quoting and paraphrasing Libet, in Raymond Tallis, *Aping Mankind: Neuromania, Darwinitis, and the Misrepresentation of Humanity* (Durham, UK: Acumen Publishing, 2011), 56.

11. The problem with that stance is that the "*refusal* to exercise free will is only intelligible to you as one of your actions if you take it to be an *exercise* of your free will." Free will therefore cannot be eliminated. John R. Searle, *Freedom and Neurobiology* (New York: Columbia University Press, 2004), 43; emphasis added.

12. See Patricia Smith Churchland, *Brain-Wise: Studies in Neurophilosophy* (Cambridge, MA: MIT Press, 2002), 192–235. For a biting critique, see Tallis, *Aping Mankind*, 51–59.

13. On the distinction between mental causes and motives in the analysis of voluntary action, see, for example, G.E.M. Anscombe, *Intention* (Cambridge, MA: Harvard University Press, 1963), 16. See also Bernard Williams, *Moral Luck* (New York: Cambridge University Press, 1981), 107.

14. Gazzaniga, *Who's in Charge?* 193, 133, 137.

15. Martin Buber, "Elements of the Interhuman," in *The Knowledge of Man* (Amherst, MA: Humanity Books, 1988).

16. For Maimonides's most sustained criticism, see "Letter on Astrology," in *A Maimonides Reader*, ed. Isadore Twersky (West Orange, NJ: Behrman House, 1972), 462–73. See also Laws of Repentance 5:4; Ravad's criticism of Maimonides/apology for astrology ad loc. For the Maimonides text alone, see Isadore Twersky, ed., *A Maimonides Reader* (West Orange, NJ: Behrman House, 1972), 78.

17. A leading Jewish example of this is Solomon ibn Gabirol's *Tikkun Middot Ha-Nefesh*. See Stephen S. Wise, ed. and trans., *The Improvement of the Moral Qualities: Solomon ibn Gabirol's Ethics* (New York: Columbia University Press, 1902).

18. Quoted in David Shatz, "Judaism, Free Will, and the Genetic and Neuroscientific Revolutions," in *Judaism, Science, and Moral Responsibility*, ed. Yitzhak Berger and David Shatz (Lanham, MD: Rowman and Littlefield, 2006), 69. A blunt statement of God's involvement in the activities of daily life may be found in Psalms 127:1–2: "Unless the LORD builds the house, its builders labor on it in vain; unless the LORD watches over the city, the watchman keeps vigil in vain. In vain do you rise early and stay up late, you who toil for the bread you eat; He provides as much for His loved ones while they sleep."

19. See Esther 4:14, where Mordecai urges Esther to act to save her peo-

ple. If she does not act, "relief and deliverance will come to the Jews from another quarter, while you and your father's house will perish. And who knows, perhaps you have attained to the royal position for just such a crisis." The plot is driven by human initiative, but its many coincidences reveal direction from "another quarter."

20. Nahum M. Sarna, *Exploring Exodus* (New York: Schocken Books, 1986), 65; emphasis added. Exegetes like Naḥmanides see the heart hardening per se as the pharaoh's punishment. That is, his punishment is precisely the suspension of his ability to freely change his mind. Naḥmanides cites a midrash to make his point:

> *For I have hardened his heart* (Exod. 10:1) Rabbi Yohanan said, "This provides a pretext for the heretics to say that God did not allow Pharaoh to repent." Rabbi Shimon ben Lakish said, "The mouths of the heretics be closed! Only, *at scoffers, He scoffs* [Prov. 3:34]. When He warns someone on three occasions and he does not turn from his ways, He closes the door of repentance on him in order to punish him for his sin. Such was the case with wicked Pharaoh. After the Holy One, blessed be He, sent him five times [the request to let His people go] and he paid no attention to His words, the Holy One, blessed be He, said to him: 'You have stiffened your neck and hardened your heart; I will double your defilement.'"

For analysis, see Alan Mittleman, "Free Choice and Determinism in Jewish Thought: An Overview," in *Neuroscience and Free Will*, ed. Robert Pollack (New York: Center for the Study of Science and Religion, Columbia University, 2009), http://www.columbia.edu/cu/cssr/ebook/FreeWill_eBook .pdf (accessed June 4, 2014).

21. For a less ambiguous, more deterministic statement, see B. Ḥullin 7b: "No man bruises his finger here on earth unless it was so decreed against him in heaven."

22. The saying "All is in the hands of heaven except the fear of heaven" occurs in three separate places in the Talmud (Berakhot 33b, Niddah 16b, and Megillah 25a). At Niddah 16b, the context is a story about the angel ("Night") in charge of conception who brings each drop of sperm before God and asks what its fate will be. God decides whether the individual resulting from the drop will be strong or weak, wise or foolish, rich or poor, but not whether they will be righteous or wicked; those latter characteristics are not in the hands of heaven. For the Jewish and Islamic career of this line

of thinking, see Alexander Altmann, "Free Will and Predestination in Saadia, Baḥya, and Maimonides," in *Essays in Jewish Intellectual History* (Hanover, NH: University of New England Press, 1981), 43.

23. Part of ibn Gabirol's point in distinguishing between a pure, free, rational soul and a composite, deterministic sense-based character is to account for individuality. Given the rational soul, all human beings would be alike, if that were all there were to us. The sense-based characteristics account for individuality in a naturalistic way.

24. Wise, *Improvement of the Moral Qualities*, 37. For selections from Judah ibn Tibbon's Hebrew translation from ibn Gabirol's original Arabic with a modern scholarly introduction and commentary, see Isaiah Tishbi and Joseph Dan, eds., *Hebrew Ethical Literature* [in Hebrew] (Jerusalem: M. Newman Publishing, 1970), 84.

25. Although ibn Gabirol is wide of the mark in ascribing higher-order traits to the senses, he is, in a way, prescient in understanding them as active shapers of experience rather than passive collectors of "sense data." Summarizing contemporary theories of visual perception, Lenn E. Goodman and D. Gregory Caramenico observe, "But the order and simplicity in what we do see is mind-made. Eyes, nerves, and brain collaborate. There's bottom-up information flow, from retina to cortex; top-down, from higher to lower cortical levels, all the way back to the movements of the eye itself, constantly scanning and readjusting, refreshing and renewing the signal; and lateral flow, within each of the six tiers of cortical cells, reconciling our variant views of the shapes and features of things, allowing us to frame coherent images—a feat that mere associative linkage of sense-data would be powerless to perform." Lenn E. Goodman and D. Gregory Caramenico, *Coming to Mind: The Soul and Its Body* (Chicago: University of Chicago Press, 2014), 56.

26. Quoted in Wise, *Improvement of the Moral Qualities*, 44–45.

27. Baḥya is an eclectic thinker. One of his influences is neo-Platonism, in which the mind represents a higher emanation of divinity than the soul. Baḥya ben Joseph ibn Pakuda, *The Book of Direction to the Duties of the Heart*, trans. Menachem Mansoor (Oxford: Littman Library of Jewish Civilization, 2004), 199.

28. Ibid., 209, 210.

29. Searle writes similarly (without the theistic claim, of course) about the phenomenological basis of our belief in free will. Whereas we sense no gap in perception—I see my hand before me without having to do anything

except look—we do sense a series of gaps in decision. I decide among alternatives, but my decision has not yet led to an action (gap one); once I have decided, I still have to initiate an action (gap two); once I have initiated an action, I have to sustain it if it requires continuity (gap three). Our first-person experience of the gaps differentiates willing from other mental events and gives rise to the feeling that we have free will. John R. Searle, *Mind: A Brief Introduction* (New York: Oxford University Press, 2004), 151–54.

30. Baḥya, *Book of Direction to the Duties of the Heart*, 211.

31. Ibid., 211–12.

32. Lenn E. Goodman, *Jewish and Islamic Philosophy: Crosspollinations in the Classical Age* (New Brunswick, NJ: Rutgers University Press, 1999), 70, 76.

33. Altmann, "Free Will and Predestination," 46.

34. Baḥya, *Book of Direction to the Duties of the Heart*, 212.

35. Laws of Repentance 5:1, quoted in Isadore Twersky, ed., *A Maimonides Reader* (West Orange, NJ: Behrman House, 1972), 75. I have changed "free will" in Twersky's translation to "freedom of choice" to render Maimonides's reshut. The latter term is the one used in Avot 3:19, "all is foreseen but reshut is given."

36. Twersky, *A Maimonides Reader*, 379; emphasis added. See also Moses Maimonides, *The Guide of the Perplexed*, trans. Shlomo Pines (Chicago: University of Chicago Press, 1963), 1:34, 3:8.

37. Goodman, *Jewish and Islamic Philosophy*, 182.

38. Twersky, *A Maimonides Reader*, 472.

39. Quoted in ibid., 382, 383.

40. Maimonides, *Guide of the Perplexed*, 2:48. For a review, see Altmann, "Free Will and Determinism," 54–58. Altmann himself is persuaded of this interpretation. Goodman rejects it. For him, the framework of Aristotelian naturalism in which Maimonides develops his views is capacious enough to accommodate voluntary human purposes.

41. Quoted in Altmann, "Free Will and Determinism," 56.

42. Scholars who hold this view include Pines and Altmann. For an analysis, see Arthur Hyman, "Aspects of the Medieval Jewish and Islamic Discussion of 'Free Choice,'" in *Freedom and Moral Responsibility: General and Jewish Perspectives*, ed. Charles H. Manekin and Menachem Kellner (College Park: University Press of Maryland, 1997), 133–52.

43. Goodman, *Jewish and Islamic Philosophy*, 182.

44. Crescas employs a distinction worked out in Al-Farabi and Avicenna among three kinds of things: that which is necessary in itself, that which is possible in itself, and that which is possible in itself but necessary due to another. See Seymour Feldman, "Crescas' Theological Determinism," *Daat* 9 (Summer 1982): 16. For Avicenna's distinction between the causes of a thing making it necessary, despite it never being necessary in and of itself, see Lenn E. Goodman, *Avicenna* (Ithaca, NY: Cornell University Press, 2006), 66.

45. For a translation of the relevant portions of *The Light of the Lord*, see Charles Manekin, ed., *Medieval Jewish Philosophical Writings* (Cambridge: Cambridge University Press, 2007), 192–235. The Hebrew original exists in an annotated edition; see Yehuda Eisenberg, ed., *Ha-R'shut Netunah* (Jerusalem: Ha-Sekhel, 1972). For a scholarly synopsis and analysis, see Warren Zev Harvey, *Physics and Metaphysics in Hasdai Crescas* (Amsterdam: J. C. Gieben, 1998).

46. Harvey, *Physics and Metaphysics*, 143, 152. For the Crescas text, see Manekin, *Medieval Jewish Philosophical Writings*, 221–22. I have given Crescas an epistemological interpretation—that is, I have resolved his view into a matter of the perspective from which one *knows* about a causal sequence. But Crescas means something more; he wants to give an analysis of the way things are *in themselves*. Working from Avicenna's distinctions between the possible and necessary, Crescas considers the existence of contingent objects—things that may not have existed, but do happen to exist—as possible in themselves. That is, their existence is not necessitated by their essence; they are not necessary beings, as God is a necessary being. They just happen to exist. A chain of causes, though, necessitated their existence, since it just happened to bring them into existence. Thus, Crescas claims that one or another set of causal factors, for example, always determines the will, but that the will per se—that is, the capacity for judgment and decision—is not determined. Here he may be criticized for conflating the will as a concept (pure potential or possibility) with the will in its actual deployments (always necessitated).

47. Manekin, *Medieval Jewish Philosophical Writings*, 224.

48. Ibid., 223.

49. Ibid., 231.

50. Donald Davidson, in a famous paper, argued that reasons are causes, and that rational explanations are a kind of causal explanation. He rejects a strong dichotomy between reasons and causes. Davidson, however, seems to

support the integrity or irreducibility of reasons, intentions, beliefs, and so on, but finds grounds to classify them as causes, or at least, classify the statements that express them as causal-explanatory statements. That seems to me to be different from approaches that view reasons, intentions, and so forth, to be reducible to physical processes, such as neural activity. See Donald Davidson, "Actions, Reasons, and Causes," *Journal of Philosophy* 60, no. 23 (November 1963): 685–700.

51. This analysis follows Searle, *Freedom and Neurobiology*, 53. (The reason, pace Davidson, may be a cause—but it doesn't cease thereby to be or function as a reason.)

52. J. L. Austin, "A Plea for Excuses," in *Philosophical Papers* (Oxford: Oxford University Press, 1970), 175–204.

CHAPTER 4: PERSONS TOGETHER

1. Aristotle, *The Politics*, trans. T. A. Sinclair (Middlesex: Penguin Books, 1970), 29; emphasis added.

2. Hannah Arendt, *The Human Condition* (Chicago: University of Chicago Press, 1958).

3. Michael Walzer asserts, "The Bible is, above all, a religious book, but it is also a political book." He adds, though, that "there is no political theory in the Bible. Political theory is a Greek invention. Nor is there a clear conception of an autonomous or distinct political realm, nor of an activity called politics, nor of a status resembling Greek citizenship.... The Biblical writers are engaged with politics but they are in an important sense ... not interested in politics." Michael Walzer, *In God's Shadow: Politics in the Hebrew Bible* (New Haven, CT: Yale University Press, 2012), xii. Poles apart from this view is that of Yoram Hazony, who sees in the biblical telling of history a full-blown political theory addressed, as in Greek thought, to questions of a general order. See Yoram Hazony, *The Philosophy of Hebrew Scripture* (New York: Cambridge University Press, 2012), 140–60. Part of this dispute is semantic, but Walzer is on to something.

4. Alexander Heidel, *The Babylonian Genesis* (Chicago: University of Chicago Press, 1967), 48–49.

5. For a development of the idea of ancient politics representing a cosmic or transcendent order, see Eric Voegelin, *The New Science of Politics: An Introduction* (Chicago: University of Chicago Press, 1952), 54–59.

6. For a study of Nimrod as the rabbinic myth of political founding, see

Alan Mittleman, *The Scepter Shall Not Depart from Judah: Perspectives on the Persistence of the Political in Judaism* (Lanham, MD: Lexington Books, 2000), 91–105. See also *Pirke de Rabbi Eliezer*, chapter 24, quoted in Hayim Nahman Bialik and Yehoshua Hana Rivinitsky, *Sefer ha-Aggada* [in Hebrew] (Tel Aviv: Dvir Publishing House, 1973), 22.

7. Walzer, *In God's Shadow*, 71.

8. Rabbinic thought develops the theme of the Tower of Babel as a rebellion against God. See B. Sanhedrin 109a.

9. Tosefta Avoda Zara 9:4; Sanhedrin 56a–b. For an encyclopedic, highly philosophical study of the Noahide Laws, see David Novak, *The Image of the Non-Jew in Judaism: The Idea of Noahide Law* (Oxford: Littman Library of Jewish Civilization, 2011); David Novak, *Natural Law in Judaism* (Cambridge: Cambridge University Press, 1998).

10. The interpretation of the significance of this story follows Hazony, *Philosophy of Hebrew Scripture*, 147–49.

11. For a comprehensive historical analysis of the links between biblical covenantalism and the Western political tradition, including the social contract tradition, see Daniel J. Elazar, *The Covenant Tradition in Politics*, 4 vols. (Rutgers, NJ: Transaction Publishers, 1997). For a philosophical approach, see David Novak, *The Jewish Social Contract: An Essay in Political Theology* (Princeton, NJ: Princeton University Press, 2005).

12. For a study of the dynamics of consent in biblical and rabbinic thought as well as in general political theory, see Mittleman, *Scepter Shall Not Depart from Judah*, 71–90.

13. Jon Levenson has argued that the daily recitation of the Shema in the liturgy is the rabbinic form of covenant renewal. Jon Levenson, *Sinai and Zion: An Entry into the Jewish Bible* (New York: Harper and Row, 1985), 83.

14. Aristotle's teachings on wealth versus moneymaking, work, and property are found in book I, especially chapters 8–10 of *Politics*, 38–47. For a philosophical analysis of the distinction between the household/economic life and public/political sphere, see Arendt, *Human Condition*, 28–37.

15. The Talmud (B. Pesaḥim 118a), commenting on this verse, has it that Adam was disconsolate when he thought that he would no longer be able to work the land, as it would only produce thorns and thistles. But when he found out that he could grow crops at the cost of his sweat, he welcomed his fate.

16. The idea that humanity furthers the work of creation by taking responsibility for the world and bringing sanctity to it through action is found, for example, in how *Sefer Ha-Hinukh* treats the commandment of circumcision. This anonymous medieval commentary on the commandments regards circumcision as a perfecting of the form of man's body. God has left creation incomplete; it requires completion/perfection (*tashlum*) through human agency. *Sefer Ha-Hinukh,* sv *Lekh L'kha.*

17. Joseph Isaac Lifshitz, *Raza d'Shabbat* [in Hebrew] (Jerusalem: Shalem Press, 2010), 11.

18. For a comprehensive overview of rabbinic economic teaching, see Meir Tamari, *With All Your Possessions: Jewish Ethics and Economic Life* (New York: Free Press, 1987). Tamari writes as a halakhically literate economist. For an equally comprehensive treatment that is far more alert to the moral philosophical and political theory implications of Jewish economic thought, see Joseph Isaac Lifshitz, *Judaism, Law, and the Free Market: An Analysis* (Grand Rapids, MI: Acton Institute, 2012). The following discussion is indebted to Lifshitz's interpretation.

19. Lifshitz, *Judaism, Law, and the Free Market,* 12–13.

20. Ibid., 14.

21. John Locke, *Two Treatises of Government,* ed. Peter Laslett (Cambridge: Cambridge University Press, 1994) 290.

22. B. Sanhedrin 64b; Rashi sv *lo yiyeh.*

23. See Moses Maimonides, "Laws of Gifts to the Poor," in *Mishneh Torah,* chapter 8.

24. See especially B. Ketubot 67b; Maimonides, "Laws of Gifts to the Poor," chapter 7; *Shulḥan Arukh,* Yoreh Deah, Hilkhot Tz'daka, para. 247–59.

25. Reuven Hammer, trans., *Sifre: A Tannaitic Commentary on the Book of Deuteronomy,* Yale Judaica Series (New Haven, CT: Yale University Press, 1986), 24:161–62 (Piska 116).

26. Maimonides, "Laws of Gifts to the Poor," chapter 9:1–3, quoted in Tamari, *With All Your Possessions,* 257.

27. Steven Pinker, *The Blank Slate: The Modern Denial of Human Nature* (New York: Penguin Books, 2002), 284–85.

28. Max Weber, *Ancient Judaism* (Glencoe, IL: Free Press, 1952), 77.

29. Frans de Waal, *Primates and Philosophers: How Morality Evolved* (Princeton, NJ: Princeton University Press, 2006), 15.

30. Ibid., 29.

31. George Kateb, *Human Dignity* (Cambridge, MA: Harvard University Press, 2011), 17.

32. Citation and subsequent sentence from de Waal, *Primates and Philosophers*, 54.

33. Carl Schmitt, *Political Theology*, trans. George Schwab (Chicago: University of Chicago Press, 2005), xv.

34. De Waal, Ibid., 55.

CONCLUSION

1. See Hans Jonas, *The Imperative of Responsibility* (Chicago: University of Chicago Press, 1985).

2. Jürgen Habermas, *The Future of Human Nature* (Cambridge, UK: Polity Press, 2003).

3. Ibid., 28, 21.

4. George Kateb, *Human Dignity* (Cambridge, MA: Harvard University Press, 2011), 25.

Index

Index

Crescas, Hasdai, 125, 136–41, 144; and Avicenna, 206n44, 206n46

Crick, Francis, 24–25, 109, 190n8

Damasio, Antonio, 102, 195n37

Darwin, Charles, 3, 12, 31, 190n8. *See also* evolution

David (king), 158

Davidson, Donald, 144, 206n50

Dawkins, Richard, 15

de Waal, Frans, 173–74, 176

Dennett, Daniel, 3, 104

depression, 107–8

Descartes, René, 7, 65; critics of, 195n37; on free will, 112–14

determinism, 111, 121, 133

Deuteronomy, 119, 121; on commitment, 67; on kingship, 152; on property, 165–69

divorce, 124–25, 171

d'mut, 51–52, 54, 191n10

Dostoyevsky, Fyodor, 183

Ecclesiastes, 56–57, 96–98, 193n22, 200n83

Elazar, Daniel J., 172

empiricism, 23–24, 34, 112, 195n37

Enuma Elish, 148–49

evolution, 5, 63, 104; and aggression, 86–87; and cosmogony, 48; and Darwin, 12, 31, 190n8; and free will, 116; and sociality, 172–77

Exodus, 92, 158–59, 164

Ezekiel, 51, 120–21

Fox, Michael, 200n83

Frankfurt, Harry, 113, 115, 189n26

free will, 58–64, 107–41; Crick on, 109; Descartes on, 112–14; Gazzaniga on, 115, 117–18, 144; Hume on, 112–13, 115, 144; Kant on, 131; medieval views

of, 125–41, 144; Nagel on, 136; neuroscientific view of, 9–10, 110, 114–18, 142–44; Rashi on, 123–24; Searle on, 204n29; E. O. Wilson on, 109–10

Freud, Sigmund, 128, 191n8

friendship, 86, 95–96, 146–47, 176

Galen, 125

Gamliel, Rabban, 164

Garr, W. Randall, 51, 192n14

Gazzaniga, Michael, 104; on free will, 115, 117–18, 144

Gersonides, 192n19

Goodman, Lenn E., 136, 185n7, 204n25, 205n40

Goshen-Gottstein, Alon, 53, 191n13

Green, Joel B., 196n43

Grotius, Hugo, 156

Habermas, Jürgen, 178–79, 181

halakha, 38, 54–55, 198n59, 209n18; Albo on, 74; death penalty in, 182

Hasdai Crescas, 76

Hazony, Yoram, 207n3

Heschel, Abraham Joshua, 18, 19, 186n10; on personhood, 23–25, 102

Higgs boson, 16

Hillel, 54, 57, 169–70

Hippocrates, 107

Hobbes, Thomas, 46–47, 89, 171, 177

homosexuality, 83–84, 199n73

Ḥoni the Circle-Maker, 145–47

hubris, 32, 155

human rights, 16, 31, 47, 194n33

Hume, David, 65, 195n37; on free will, 112–13, 115, 144

humoral medicine, 119, 126

ibn Gabirol, Solomon, 125–28, 133, 202n17, 204nn23–25

immigration policies, 2